APOLLO
TO
THE
MOON

A HISTORY IN 50 OBJECTS

APOLLO
TO THE
MOON

TEASEL MUIR-HARMONY

Foreword by **MICHAEL COLLINS**, Apollo 11 Astronaut

NATIONAL
GEOGRAPHIC

Washington, D.C.

Contents

PAGES 2–3: Harrison Schmitt of Apollo 17 stands near the lunar rover, parked on the edge of Shorty crater, in a panorama created with several photographs taken by Mission Commander Eugene Cernan.

OPPOSITE: Apollo 4, a crewless test mission, awaits launch at Kennedy Space Center in November 1967.

Foreword

Michael Collins
Astronaut (1963–1970), Gemini 10 pilot
and Apollo 11 command module pilot
Director, Smithsonian National Air and
Space Museum, 1971–78

Fondly I recall wandering the halls of the National Air and Space Museum when I was director there in the 1970s and eavesdropping on visiting families. I wanted to know what was on their minds, and I was almost always rewarded with "Daddy, is it real?" "Absolutely, Virginia, the museum's artifacts *are* real, and that is what makes them important and interesting." Some parts of a flight cannot be constructed here on the ground. For example, John Glenn's orbital view of the planet was riveting, but cannot be experienced on Earth. Yet the visitors there get a close second, seeing his actual camera. It is real, and you almost get the feeling you were there with him as he peered through the viewfinder.

Later, photographs from the Apollo program were not only beautiful but have great historical importance as well. Perhaps a quick review of those missions would help bring these photographs into focus. Apollo started with a disaster, fire inside the command module in a ground test that killed Gus Grissom, Ed White, and Roger Chaffee. Later named Apollo 1, it was followed by Apollo 2 through 6, unmanned tests required to prepare for people on board.

Apollo 7: Wally Schirra, Walt Cunningham, Donn Eisele tested the command and service modules for 10 days in Earth orbit.

Apollo 8: Frank Borman, Jim Lovell, and Bill Anders were the first to reach escape velocity, in a daring visit to lunar orbit.

Apollo 9: Jim McDivitt, Dave Scott, and Rusty Schweickart tested the lunar module in Earth orbit.

Apollo 10: Tom Stafford, John Young, and Gene Cernan completed a lunar orbit dress rehearsal for the first landing.

PAGE 6: Michael Collins stands in front of Lunar Module 2, on display at the Smithsonian National Air and Space Museum, during his time as the museum's director.

OPPOSITE: Michael Collins took this photo of the Apollo 11 lunar module through the command module window. He commented that every living human is captured in frame, except himself, and gave it the name "Three Billion Plus Two."

Apollo 11: Finally, on July 20, 1969, this mission landed on the moon as President Kennedy had ordered in 1961.

Following were flights 12 through 17, expanding our knowledge of the moon. Once past Apollo 1, the sequence was truly amazing, one success after another. As an experienced test pilot, I expected a lot more trouble once we started flying. The two most important flights, I believe, were Apollo 8 and Apollo 11—8 about *leaving* and 11 about *arriving*. A hundred years from now, when historians consider the Earth-moon duo, they may argue about which of the steps was more difficult or more important.

That question will not be answered by examining a photo from each flight, either one of which, I believe, has left its mark on the human psyche. First is Bill Anders's Hasselblad shot of the tiny Earth as it pops up over the lunar horizon, the first time a human took such a photo. The other is Neil Armstrong's take of Buzz Aldrin on the lunar surface, with the unexpected dividend of Neil himself visible in reflection from the visor of Buzz's helmet.

I join these two, claiming a place in history with my favorite photo, of Neil and Buzz in their lunar module *Eagle* as they return from the surface to me orbiting the moon in *Columbia*. *Eagle* is only half there (just the ascent stage; the descent stage being left on the moon), but it looks proud of itself. It is slightly below me but lined up perfectly with Earth, which is a few degrees above the horizon. I have dubbed this picture "Three Billion Plus Two," and today it lives just above my desk. Even now I get a warm feeling when I look at it. But much as I do, I think in general I like to look at art even more. Strange as it may seem surrounded by priceless artifacts in the Air and Space Museum, the art gallery was my favorite spot to slow down and take some time to think about what I was seeing.

Art takes us one step beyond photography, past the lens into the imagination. And one can argue that leaving the surface of Earth allows the imagination to expand a bit. Certainly amazing results come from the artists who have watched launches or spent a lot of time in balloons or airplanes. In space art, Chesley Bonestell is my favorite for

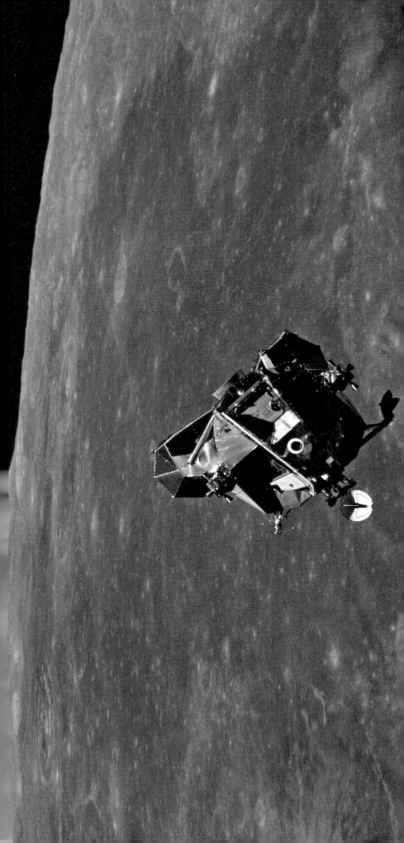

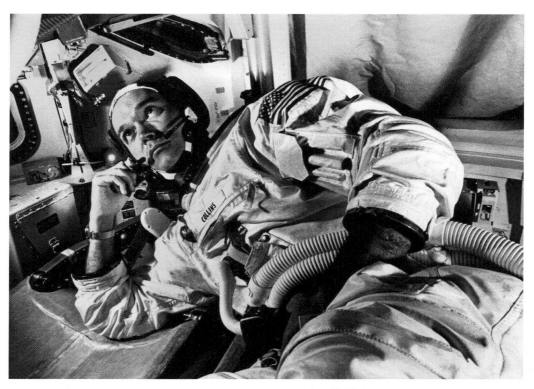

imagining the places we have never visited, while two with space experience, Alexei Leonov, and my good friend and fellow astronaut, Alan Bean, have produced remarkable paintings.

One lesser known figure is James Dean, who is an extremely talented artist, and who was employed by the museum for many years as curator of art. Jim, because of his own reputation, was able to acquire paintings from his many friends, among them Jamie Wyeth and Robert Rauschenberg.

After the flight of Apollo 11, when I was leaving *Columbia* for the last time, it didn't seem right to simply walk away, without a trace of my eight days aboard. Inanimate object though it was, I wanted it to remember me somehow. So I went down into the navigation station, which seemed like the brains of the place, and paid it this compliment: "Spacecraft 107—alias Apollo 11—alias Columbia. The best ship to come down the line. God Bless Her. Michael Collins, CMP." After writing that on a panel, I felt better about leaving.

Photographs, art, even graffiti: They come alive because of what they represent. But three-dimensional objects, *artifacts* as we call them, are what set a museum apart from other institutions. They are the heart and soul of a museum.

I'm sure not everyone wants to fly into space, and even those who do, can't—except the lucky few. But those left behind still seem fascinated. I have been asked hundreds of times, "What is it really like up there?" I can often get by with "cool" or "awesome," but then I am disappointed that I haven't given a better, more evocative, reply. Maybe if I were standing next to *Columbia,* I could. The magic of a museum is that, using artifacts and their supporting materials to bring visitors into the story, to show vividly what it was really like up there. Among museums, the National Air and Space Museum is especially blessed by having been able to acquire an incomparable collection, from the Wright Flyer to the space shuttle. Beyond that, as demonstrated in this fine book, the curators have displayed their exceptional expertise in organizing these national treasures into fascinating exhibits. •

1 Plaque: Wright Brothers' Airplane and Apollo 11

Date: 1903; 1969
Manufacturer: Wilbur and Orville Wright; Neil Armstrong
Origin: Kitty Hawk, North Carolina; the moon
Materials: Wood, fabric, cardboard, paper, plastic, metal screws
Dimensions: Overall: 13³/₁₆ by ¹³/₁₆ by 7½ inches; Wood shard: ½ by 1³/₁₆ inches; Fabric: 3½ by 4 inches

On December 17, 1903, on a windy beach in North Carolina, the Wright brothers achieved the first power-controlled flight. Pieces of their plane—fabric and a wood shard—took another historic flight more than 60 years later, from "Kittyhawk to Tranquility Base," as the plaque (opposite) reads. Neil Armstrong brought these pieces of the Wright Flyer with him aboard the lunar module *Eagle,* when he landed on the moon in July 1969. The wood was taken from the left propeller, and the fabric from the upper left wing after a gust of wind damaged the airplane following its fourth flight.

Before Apollo 11, Armstrong made a special agreement with the National Museum of the U.S. Air Force in Dayton, Ohio, to include the Wright Flyer's fabric and wood shard in his personal preference kit. NASA issued all astronauts one small bag for personal or small items they wanted to carry into space. Most were filled with miniature flags, family jewelry, mission medallions, patches, and other mementos. Buzz Aldrin packed a tiny vial of wine and a wafer to take Communion on the moon. But of all the items Armstrong brought, he was most proud of the pieces of the Wright Flyer.

This wood shard and scrap of fabric elicit an important question: Why have artifacts been, and continue to be, essential connections to the past?

Fragments of the 1903 Wright Flyer, which Neil Armstrong
brought with him to the moon, along with letters of
authenticity from Armstrong and the Wright estate

For Armstrong, bringing along these artifacts with his limited personal belongings honored pioneering aviators. It also bound together two events separated by many decades. Pieces of wood and fabric connected the first lunar landing with the first airplane flight, drawing a thread between two critical moments in aerospace history.

Now, half a century after the first moon landing, these artifacts connect us to Armstrong. They speak to his priorities, his identity as a pilot, his thought-fulness, and his sense of duty. We can imagine Armstrong agreeing to carry pieces of the Wright Flyer on the mission, recognizing the historical weight of such a gesture. We can imagine him placing this fabric and wood in his personal preference kit, packing the Beta cloth bag securely aboard *Eagle,* ensuring its safe landing on the moon. We can imagine him taking them out after the flight, holding them in his hand, and writing the letter of authentication, which forever cemented the moon

landing as the next great moment in the history of flight.

Like Armstrong, this book recognizes the significance and power of artifacts. Tangible, real objects can connect the past to our present. Fifty years from the first lunar landing, the 50 objects in these pages let us revisit a remarkable moment in American history, when grand ambitions overcame grand obstacles, and allow us not only to understand the moment anew but to make it part of our lives. In this book, you will find some of the most evocative artifacts of the Apollo era. They help tell the full story of spaceflight by revealing the tangle of technological, political, cultural, and social dimensions of the Apollo missions. They evoke questions about how the objects were made, who made them, and how they were used. The objects bear the physical marks of their history, prompting insights and providing evidence about the past. They can commemorate achievements and provoke revaluations of history.

Project Apollo ranks among the most bold, challenging, and inspiring undertakings of the 20th century. In less than a decade, the United States leaped from suborbital spaceflight to landing humans on the moon and returning them safely to Earth. When President John F. Kennedy proposed Project Apollo in May 1961, he had been in office for just over four months. Only one American, astronaut Alan Shepard, had flown in space (object #6). Over the following eight years, the U.S. space program developed new capabilities, facilities, and managerial practices. Project Apollo mobilized a workforce of NASA employees and contractors in the hundreds of thousands, established a global satellite-tracking network, and invested in the research and development of innovative technologies. It cost five times more than the Manhattan Project, and more than twice what the government spent on the Panama Canal, and became the most expensive government-funded civilian technological program in U.S. history, at one point accounting for more than 4 percent of the federal budget.

It would be hard to overstate how unique the "Apollo moment" was. The United States and the Soviet Union were locked in fierce competition for global influence. American concerns over the widespread reactions to the launch of Sputnik in 1957 were only heightened by the Soviet success of the first crewed mission in April 1961 (object #4). Spaceflight signified leadership, and the United States was falling behind. President Kennedy chose the moon not only as the destination but also as the answer to the question of how to secure geopolitical alignment. And within the context of a booming postwar economy, the scientific and technological optimism of the day, and in response to Soviet space capability, this large-scale presidentially directed undertaking was able to move from the realm of science fiction to science fact.

Between 1958 and 1963, the first U.S. human spaceflight program—Project Mercury—sent astronauts on suborbital and orbital missions in one-person spacecraft. Next, Project Gemini tested capabilities that would be necessary for lunar exploration, like rendezvous and docking over the course of 10 missions. Then, starting in 1968, Project Apollo sent 24 people to the moon. Between 1969 and 1972, 12 of these people planted their feet on the lunar surface. The number of "firsts" achieved are too numerous to list, and many of them have not been matched since. Project Apollo did not just create the largest rocket ever built, or achieve the greatest distance ever traveled by humans—it affected the lives of billions of people in nearly every community on every continent.

The material legacy of Apollo is immense. From capsules to space suits to the ephemera of life aboard a spacecraft, the Smithsonian Institution national collection comprises thousands of artifacts.

This carefully curated selection of 50 of these objects reveals how Project Apollo touched people's lives, both within the space program and around the world. More than space hardware alone, the artifacts featured in these pages reflect the most recent historical scholarship, which explores the deep interconnection between Project Apollo and broader developments in American society and politics. The objects in these pages are not only monuments to achievements in spaceflight but also access points to the complexities of this history.

For decades, our understanding of Project Apollo primarily centered on the development of technology, the feats of astronauts, and the celebration of human achievement. In the late 1980s, an increasing number of historians started investigating the social, political, and cultural significance of Apollo, gaining insights into the historical implications and consequences of this unprecedented program. Now, 50 years after the first lunar landing, it is an opportune moment to reassess the history and legacy of Project Apollo. The artifacts of Apollo help us do just that.

The first artifact in Section 1—the crumpled Vanguard satellite (object #2)—is a potent physical illustration of U.S. stature at the beginning of the space age. The initial failure of the Vanguard launch, in part, put the country and President Kennedy on a trajectory to invest in sending men to the moon. Although a fledgling space agency, established in 1958, NASA overcame extraordinary technological and managerial challenges to advance human spaceflight, as highlighted in Section 2. The multistage Apollo spacecraft, featured in Section 3, not only required revolutionary engineering complexity and precision but also performed flawlessly through the program.

As the artifacts within these pages reveal, Apollo was a human endeavor, on a human scale. Sending men to the moon shaped the social and cultural history of the United States and the world, as people both engaged with and protested against American spaceflight. The Southern Christian Leadership Conference (SCLC) contribution can (object #20) in Section 4 is a visceral reminder of the critique of government spending on space exploration. Section 5 emphasizes the human side of Project Apollo through artifacts like astronaut Mike Collins's off-the-shelf razor and shaving cream (object #22). As a personal item, it illustrates not only the lived experiences of participants in the Apollo program but also the many ways program planners had to improvise with what was available to meet Kennedy's deadline. The urine collection device (object #23) silently reminds us of the exclusion of women from the Apollo astronaut corps.

With the world watching, Walter Cronkite used the lunar module model (object #26) in Section 6, to explain the Apollo 11 astronauts' path in July 1969. The six crews that traversed the lunar surface between 1969 and 1972 set up experiments and collected samples that advanced our understanding of the moon and our solar system. One of the scientific instruments featured in Section 7, the ultraviolet camera from the Apollo 16 mission (object #34), enables us to learn about the biography of George Carruthers, a pioneering African-American physicist at NASA who overcame racial

NASA produced this detailed schematic of the Apollo lunar mission profile in 1967. It shows every major step of the mission, from launch and lunar orbit to the return to Earth.

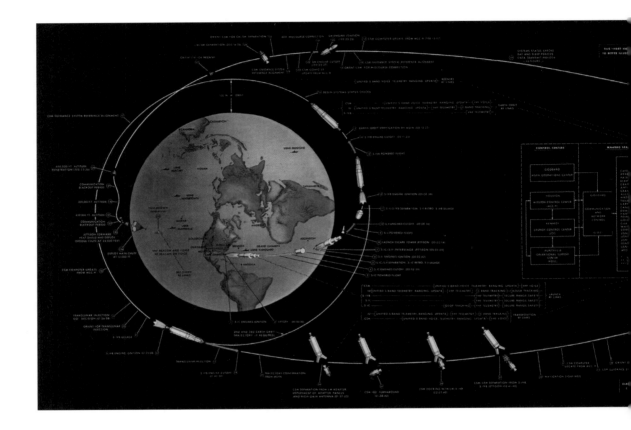

prejudice to make a major contribution to science. The return to Earth inspired both innovative technology, like the Apollo 16 parachute (object #45), as well as an outpouring of recognition and honors like the Japanese tour medal (object #48), featured in Section 9.

The artifacts in these pages also speak to the scale of Project Apollo. Look at the "origin" line in each artifact essay. Components that sent humans to the moon originated from across the country, and around the world. The Saturn V rocket parts ranged from the instrument ring (object #13), manufactured in Huntsville, Alabama, to the massive F1 engines (object #50) from Rocketdyne factories in Los Angeles. Many artifacts came

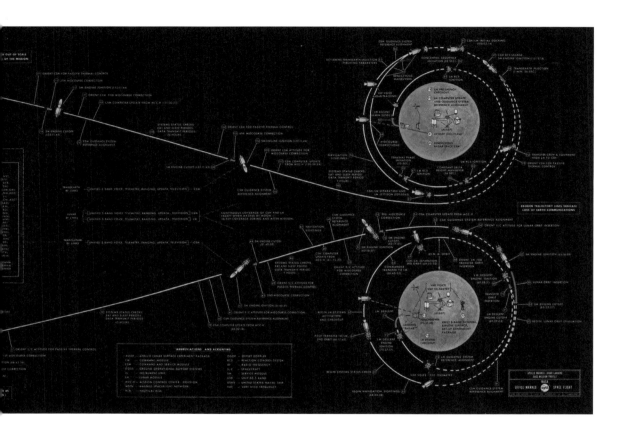

from even farther afield, like the Hasselblad camera from Sweden used on Apollo 17 (object #25). Beyond that, the media, toy companies, and foreign governments, among others, created the material legacy of Project Apollo, like RCA's cardboard visor (object #18).

Wood and fabric from the Wright Flyer connected Armstrong's first lunar landing to the first power-controlled airplane flight. Today, they can connect us to both of those moments in the history of aeronautics. Artifacts let the past become part of our lived experience. They transport us to another time and make history imaginable, even tangible. They confirm how something that once seemed impossible is within our reach. •

The Early Days

Section 1

Introduction

"If we are to win the battle . . ."

On May 25, 1961, addressing a joint session of Congress as well as a live television audience, President John F. Kennedy proposed the most audacious space program in history. "If we are to win the battle that is now going on around the world between freedom and tyranny," Kennedy urged from the House Chamber of the U.S. Capitol Building, "the dramatic achievements in space . . . should have made clear to us all . . . the impact of this adventure on the minds of men everywhere, who are attempting to make a determination of which road they should take." He continued, "Now it is time to take longer strides—time for a great new American enterprise—time for this nation to take a clearly leading role in space achievement . . ."

The new president then called for an elaborate lunar exploration program where men would land on the moon and return safely back to Earth, a goal to be reached within the decade. This unprecedented feat—more than any other, Kennedy believed—could tip the global balance of power toward the United States.

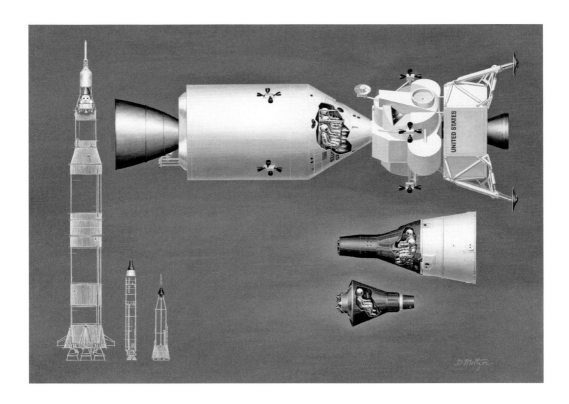

The first few years of the space race were fierce, as the Soviet Union and the United States sprinted to outdo each other. Innovation upon innovation, thrilling launches, and new possibilities all occurred in quick succession. Kennedy's proposal for Project Apollo came just four years after humans first launched a satellite into orbit, a time filled with rapid and dramatic growth. It was also a time when the United States seemed to be trailing behind the Soviet Union in space firsts, including the very public failure of the U.S. Vanguard satellite and the advent of human spaceflight by Soviet cosmonaut Yuri Gagarin. ●

2 Vanguard TV-3 Satellite

Date: Failed launch, December 6, 1957
Manufacturer: Naval Research Laboratory
Origin: Washington, D.C.
Materials: Magnesium-aluminum frame; silicon monoxide solar cells
Dimensions: Body: $9^{13}/_{19}$ by $7^{1}/_{2}$ by $7^{1}/_{2}$ inches; Arms (each): $12^{3}/_{16}$ by $^{3}/_{16}$ inches

On October 4, 1957, the Soviet Union stunned the world with the successful launch of the first artificial satellite, Sputnik 1. This impressive technological feat had broad implications for Soviet missile capability, as well as public relations clout. Fearing that political leaders and the public around the world would view Soviet communism as an appealing alternative to capitalism, American officials scrambled to prove that the United States had the technical know-how to launch its own satellite. Pushing ahead of schedule, the United States attempted a launch on December 6, 1957, of its first satellite, Vanguard (pictured opposite), which ended in humiliating defeat.

Seven years earlier, at a dinner party in the suburbs of Washington, D.C., scientists gathered at the home of James Van Allen came up with a bold plan over bites of chocolate cake. They believed the time was right to organize a large-scale study of Earth and its environment for 1957, when the sun would be most active. The International Geophysical Year (IGY), as their idea came to be known, brought professionals together from 67 nations in the largest global scientific cooperative program in history. The planning committee for the IGY called for the development of artificial satellites to support geodetic and atmospheric studies of Earth, to better determine our planet's size and shape, its orientation in space, its gravity field and atmosphere, and how this all changes

"Our main problem was the fact that Vanguard had the unique position in those early days of the space age of being a public, or basically unclassified project. Vanguard was the only 'open project,' so it bore the brunt of the national displeasure with early space failures."

—Larry G. Hastings, Project Vanguard public information officer

The White House announced the approval of a scientific satellite on July 29, 1955. The Naval Research Laboratory (NRL)'s Vanguard program won its bid to develop the American satellite for the IGY. In the following two years, the NRL developed the Viking sounding rocket into a three-stage launch vehicle, as well as constructing an international tracking system and a suite of experiments. Their planned satellite would be approximately 20 inches in diameter, with solar batteries running sensors to detect cosmic rays, magnetic fields, and radiation. The Glenn L. Martin Company, which served as the main contractor for the project, made do with a scant budget, at one point using springs removed from commercial mousetraps as components for their rocket. They were on track to launch the first satellite in March 1958.

When the Soviet Union orbited Sputnik in October 1957, then followed it with another, larger satellite with a dog on board a month later, U.S. leaders felt the threat of losing the implied space race. In

over time. The United States and the Soviet Union both took this call as an opportunity to launch satellites within a peaceful, scientific context.

the wake of Sputnik pressure, the NRL moved the launch date of Test Vehicle 3 (TV-3), which would later become known as Vanguard, up to December 1957. TV-3 was intended to be the first full test of the three-stage rocket, topped with a six-inch sphere. A more sophisticated satellite launch in March was also planned.

Four days before the launch of TV-3, spectators started arriving at the desolate beaches of Cape Canaveral. The already scanty accommodations in the area were full of reporters, tourists, and early space enthusiasts. According to the *New York Times,* local shops completely sold out of binoculars. The beleaguered engineers of Project Vanguard had an audience, with no guarantee that the test would succeed. After several delays, on the morning of December 6, 1957,

On December 6, 1957, the Vanguard TV-3 failed to launch. The satellite was nestled in the nose cone, which is just beginning to break off in this photograph.

Vanguard launched. Two seconds after ignition, having lifted only four feet, something went wrong.

The engine lost all thrust and fell back on the launchpad, rupturing the fuel tanks and engulfing the rocket in an enormous fireball. Eerily, the beeping signal of the Vanguard test satellite still sounded in the stunned control room. The next morning, photographs of the explosion were accompanied by sensationalist headlines, such as "Oh what a Flopnik! America's Sputnik dies bleeping on the ground," splashed upon front pages across the world. The satellite was quickly dubbed "Dudnik" and "Kaputnik."

Beyond embarrassment for the team, the public failure of the Vanguard launch damaged American geopolitical prestige. Many commenters blamed the Eisenhower Administration for drawing attention to what should have been a scientific test rather than a publicity event. Then Senator Lyndon Johnson soon articulated a widespread sentiment: "I shrink a little inside of me

"We managed so successfully to focus the eyes of the world on the effort that, when it exploded, the whole world was watching."

—*Nation* editorial, December 21, 1957

whenever the U.S. announces a great event and it blows up in our face."

The Army's Project Orbiter would succeed in putting the first American satellite in space with Explorer 1 in January 1958. Although both Orbiter's and Project Vanguard's next attempts would be failures, Vanguard 1 did make it to space that March. Today, the battered remains of Vanguard TV-3 materially embody the trailing position of the United States at the beginning of the space race— an embarrassing failure for the fledgling space program, but not a fatal blow. •

3 Project Moonwatch Telescope

Date: Late 1950s
Manufacturer: Unknown, possibly homemade from war surplus parts by the Smithsonian Astrophysical Observatory
Origin: United States
Materials: Aluminum and brass, with glass optics
Dimensions: 12 by 5 by 14 inches

As satellites orbit overhead, they drag through the remaining high atmosphere and sway from the varying pull of Earth's gravitational field. Tracking the oscillations in a satellite's orbit can tell us about the nature of the atmosphere, the shape and density of Earth, and how other objects—including ballistic missiles—will travel through space. But in the mid-1950s, just as there was no system able to put satellites in space, there were

no systems to track them. Dr. Fred Whipple, astronomer and director of the Smithsonian Astrophysical Observatory (SAO), came up with a solution.

Building on his earlier work spotting comets and meteors, Whipple proposed an optical tracking system, insisting that satellites should be visible overhead in the twilight. The SAO planned a series of 12 large astronomical cameras, called Baker–Nunn telescopes after their developers, which would photograph passing satellites using their speed and position in the sky to calculate their orbits. However, astronomers would need to know where to look first.

Whipple thought that the first stage in optical tracking could rely on teams of volunteers, amateur astronomers who would watch the sky at dusk and dawn, waiting to see the telltale glow of a satellite. The project was dubbed Operation Moonwatch, and volunteers using small telescopes (opposite) would create a "fence" by focusing on overlapping areas of sky, often with a pole called a

BELOW: An ideal setup for a Moonwatch team, as shown in this period illustration, included multiple observers ready to announce any satellite sightings to a radio operator.

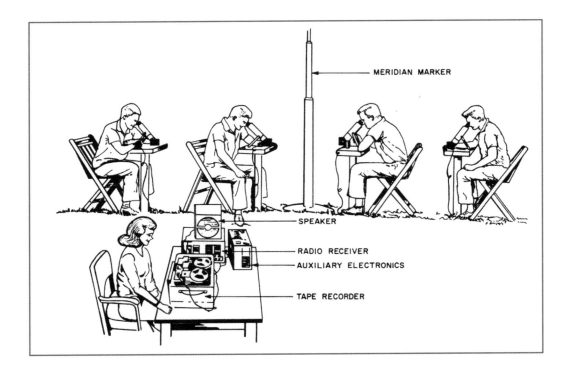

"meridian" in their view. Once observers caught sight of a satellite, they would record the time it crossed their view in relation to the meridian, as well as what stars it passed. This information was then relayed to the SAO, where it was used to calculate the object's orbit for the Baker–Nunn telescopes.

In 1956, the Smithsonian put out a worldwide call for Operation Moonwatch in "a spirit of scientific corporation." As the number of satellites increased, so did the Moonwatchers, with more than 230 teams numbering 8,000 members by 1958. Moonwatchers could buy or build the small telescopes the SAO promoted, and round off their station with basic radio equipment. The Moonwatch teams represented every walk of life, from neighborhood groups organized by astronomers and schoolteachers to teenagers training themselves. More than a third of all Moonwatchers were women, who founded and led many teams. Many volunteers became extremely adept at spotting and calculating orbits, sometimes even better than the researchers and computers at the SAO.

Outside the SAO, much of the scientific community was skeptical of the effectiveness and accuracy of the volunteer trackers. John P. Hagan, a lead scientist and radio astronomer for Project Vanguard, said, "Suppose some joker flies a plane up to 60,000 feet and throws out a golf ball. Then the plane vanishes without a trace. Can you find the golf ball? That's about the task in locating a satellite." Nonetheless, when Sputnik 1 launched October 4, 1957, Moonwatchers were at their telescopes. Not only were the volunteers of Operation Moonwatch effective, but they also became essential. In a few years, the tens of thousands of satellite observations made by amateur astronomers around the

"Let's be brutal. Moonwatch never had much love from the professionals. Satellites were going to be a quick ride to glory so why share it with a bunch of amateurs? They would not be needed, electronic stuff was much better. Ha!"

—Walter Houston, English professor, Moonwatch member

world shaped the early development of space exploration. For all the millions of dollars spent to get Vanguard and Sputnik off the ground, one of the space age's most important scientific tools was made with $30 of aluminum and surplus optics. •

4 Yuri Gagarin 10-Kopek Stamp

Date: 1961
Manufacturer: Soviet Ministry of Communications
Origin: U.S.S.R.
Materials: Paper, ink, adhesive
Dimensions: 1$\frac{11}{16}$ by 1$\frac{3}{16}$ inches

On April 12, 1961, Yuri Gagarin became the first space traveler in history. The stamp designed to celebrate the flight depicts Gagarin looking up at the stars next to a stylized rocket climbing high over the walls of the Kremlin. Colorful and elaborate stamps, with high denominations, were airmail stamps, designed to capture the attention of foreign audiences and stamp collectors, not the general Soviet public. The fictitious depiction of Gagarin's Vostok spacecraft was not simply based on aesthetic appeal: It reflects the strict secrecy surrounding the Soviet space program.

Before the flight, the Soviet Ministry of Communications prepared this stamp, along with two others in smaller denominations. They were released just a few days after the mission. The three-kopek domestic stamp, the lowest denomination, was plain, not eye-catching. The six- and 10-kopek stamps—intended for international audiences—incorporated more dramatic and attention-grabbing imagery. Stamps issued for subsequent missions followed a similar pattern: a cosmonaut portrait, the mission date, and a fictitious spacecraft.

In contrast, the U.S. four-cent domestic 1962 Project Mercury stamp illustrates an accurate Mercury capsule careening through space. Where Soviet stamps depicted imaginary spacecraft, U.S. engravers worked from engineering drawings. When the Soviet Union displayed models of the Vostok for eager exhibit-goers through the early 1960s, they intentionally hid technical details by using simplified models; as a result, specifics on the Vostok spacecraft were secret

ЧЕЛОВЕК СТРАНЫ СОВЕТОВ В КОСМОСЕ

СССР

12-IV-1961

ПОЧТА

10 к

4 c

U.S. MAN
IN SPACE

PROJECT MERCURY

"Looking at the Earth from afar, you realize it is too small for conflict and just big enough for co-operation."

—Yuri Gagarin, cosmonaut, first man in space

until 1967. Their primary concern seemed to be that if the world found out that Soviet spacecraft were designed to crash-land, with the cosmonaut ejecting from the capsule just before impact, the legitimacy of Soviet space successes could be called into question. In contrast, American astronaut John Glenn's space capsule, Friendship 7, was exhibited around the world after its flight, accompanied by technical diagrams of the Mercury spacecraft.

There was some secrecy surrounding the production of the Friendship 7 stamp, but it was of a different nature than that of the Vostok stamp. Leading up to the flight, the team working on the stamp kept it a secret, giving their colleagues the impression that they were all on vacation. The stamp designer worked from home while the engravers sneaked into the facility at night and on weekends.

As part of the effort to keep the design a surprise, the bureau sent sealed packages containing the stamps to over 300 post offices. Within minutes of the news that Glenn had landed safely in the Atlantic Ocean on February 20, 1962, they were officially released, marking the first time a U.S. stamp was issued alongside the event it was designed to commemorate. Within an hour, lines of eager collectors started forming at post offices around the country. Although the stamp itself had been kept secret, the spacecraft it depicted was widely disseminated in photographs, news coverage, and on souvenirs. Officials at NASA as well as the White House, State Department, and United States Information Agency viewed this type of openness as an illustration of the values of a democratic society. ●

5 Kennedy Debate Chair, 1960

Date: 1950s
Manufacturer/designer: PP Mobler/ Hans Wegner
Origin: Denmark
Materials: Wood, brown leather
Dimensions: 42 by 28 by 20 inches

Television ushered in a new era of political strategy. In the 1960s, public image took on a more pivotal role than ever before. Perhaps no one was more attuned to the power of public persona, and the importance of public relations, than a junior senator from Massachusetts, John Fitzgerald Kennedy. His experience in the 1960 presidential debate in particular amplified Kennedy's impression that image matters in politics. This insight would come to play a major role in his decision to send men to the moon when he became president in 1961. "No single space project in this period will be more impressive to mankind," Kennedy argued. In 1969, the first global television broadcast of the Apollo 11 mission fulfilled the president's dream of showing the world the technological and scientific prowess of the United States.

At 9:30 p.m. eastern standard time (EST) on Monday, September 26, 1960, Senator John F. Kennedy and then Vice President Richard Nixon took the stage at the CBS Studios in Chicago. Before a viewership of roughly 70 million Americans, the presidential candidates argued over domestic policy. The 1960 debate was not only the first televised debate; it was also the first time presidential candidates from the major political parties came together to face off in person. The two candidates presented a stark contrast. As CBS president Frank Stanton later observed, "Kennedy was bronzed beautifully . . . Nixon looked like death."

The youthful Kennedy also sat comfortably in this chair, displaying ease

and confidence. Nixon, in contrast, tensely grasped his chair's arm and seemed engulfed in his oversize suit, sweat collecting on his face. Both candidates spoke on their views of education, health care, the economy, and the larger Cold War context. But, as journalist David Halberstam noted, "within hours no one could recall anything that was said, only what they looked like, what they felt like."

Popular lore suggests that television viewers assumed Kennedy won the debate, while radio listeners were convinced Nixon was the victor. Although historians disagree over who actually "won," the message was clear: The image on the television screen mattered.

"I believe that this nation should commit itself to achieving the goal, before this decade is out, of landing a man on the moon and returning him safely to the earth. No single space project in this period will be more impressive to mankind, or more important for the long-range exploration of space; and none will be so difficult or expensive to accomplish."

—President Kennedy, May 25, 1961

The historical significance of the event struck CBS's Stanton strongly. He commissioned commemorative silver plates for the backs of the chairs, each inscribed with the name of the candidate who sat in the seat. The chairs used in the debate, as well as the rest of the television set, had been chosen for their forward-looking aesthetic. Famed Danish designer Hans Wegner first created the "Round Chair," in 1949. Quickly dubbed simply "the Chair," this design became a symbol of the popular Danish modern style. Stanton would later donate the chairs to the Smithsonian National Museum of American History.

Three more televised debates would follow the one in September. Each further established a new era of political strategy that put public relations at front and center. When asked if he thought he would have won the election without the help of television, Kennedy responded, "I don't think so." As historian Alan Schroeder observed, "A revolutionary programming genre burst forth that

SENATOR JOHN F. KENNEDY
USED THIS CHAIR IN
THE FIRST FACE-TO-FACE DISCUSSION
BETWEEN PRESIDENTIAL CANDIDATES
BROADCAST SEPTEMBER 26, 1960
FROM CBS TELEVISION STUDIO 1
CHICAGO

night in Chicago, one that fundamentally realigned both politics and the media in America."

Kennedy's decision to propose Project Apollo—the most expensive civilian technological program in the country's history—was rooted in his appreciation for the impact of prestige on America's geopolitical standing. For Kennedy, the *image* of national strength directly contributed to national strength. This was a lesson he appreciated while sitting in this chair in the CBS television studio in Chicago. Less than a year after the debate, Kennedy presented Project Apollo to the American people via a televised broadcast while addressing a joint session of Congress. •

APOLLO VIP

John F. Kennedy's Space Policy

It may come as a surprise that the president who launched the boldest space program in history started out as a space skeptic. John F. Kennedy's relationship to spaceflight evolved rapidly from his role as a Massachusetts senator in the 1950s to his tenure in the Oval Office in the early 1960s. One journalist observed, "Of all the major problems facing Kennedy when he came into office, he probably knew and understood least about space."

Rocket guidance pioneer Charles Stark Draper recounted how in 1957, shortly after the Soviet Union launched Sputnik, Kennedy cynically told him over drinks at Boston's storied Locke-Ober café that all rockets were a waste of money. During his presidential campaign in 1960, the candidate rarely mentioned NASA, even though he emphasized a space and missile gap. But shortly after taking office, Kennedy's attitude toward spaceflight changed dramatically.

On April 12, 1961, the Soviet Union made history by launching the first human into space, Yuri Gagarin. Like Sputnik, Gagarin's flight was a blow to America's scientific and technological standing on the world stage. Days later, the failure of the CIA-backed Bay of Pigs invasion of Cuba created another challenge to U.S. prestige. Within days, Kennedy asked Vice President Lyndon Johnson to find a "space program which promises dramatic results in which we could win." Johnson, with the aid of space experts, came back with a May 8 report to the president that made a case for landing humans on the moon. "It is man, not merely machines, in space that capture the imagination of the world," the memo explained. It continued, "If we fail to accept this challenge it may be interpreted as a lack of national vigor."

Just a few weeks later, on May 25, Kennedy addressed a joint session of Congress on the nation's urgent national needs. One of these needs, he argued, was doing something in space to demonstrate U.S. global leadership. Sending Americans to the moon and returning them safely to Earth, he emphasized, could persuade people in developing countries to choose American "freedom" over Soviet "tyranny."

NASA's budget increased by 89 percent after Kennedy's address, and by another 101 percent the following year. Project Apollo became the most expensive civilian technological program in U.S. history.

Kennedy believed that a robust space program was essential for securing the status of U.S. global leadership. He told the NASA administrator that Project Apollo should be the "top priority of the agency and except for defense, the top priority of the United States government. Otherwise, we shouldn't be spending this kind of money, because I'm not that interested in space."

Kennedy urged the country to invest in lunar exploration, and he threw his full support behind NASA, pragmatically recognizing the international relations and national security implications of winning the space race.

6 *Freedom 7* Mercury Capsule

Date: 1961
Manufacturer: McDonnell Aircraft Corp.
Origin: St. Louis, Missouri
Materials: Titanium, nickel-steel alloy, and beryllium shingles, glass fiber, resin
Dimensions: 7 feet 8 inches by 6 feet 1 inch
Weight: 2,316 pounds

On May 5, 1961, a compact one-person space capsule carried the first American into space. That morning, at 9:34 a.m. EST, Commander Alan Shepard, Jr., took his seat in his spacecraft, and a slender Redstone rocket propelled *Freedom 7* on a suborbital flight. It was quick trip—just over 15 minutes—but the spacecraft traveled at speeds of up to 5,180 miles an hour to an altitude of 116.5 miles, before land-ing in the Atlantic more than 300 miles from Cape Canaveral, Florida.

Three weeks earlier, Soviet cosmonaut Yuri Gagarin had become the first human in space, a blow to American national confidence. Before they sent a human into space, NASA launched a Mercury capsule atop a Redstone rocket with a chimpanzee named Ham inside. Because there were problems with the booster on this launch, NASA delayed Shepard's flight. If *Freedom 7* had launched on time, Shepard would have flown in space before Gagarin. Shepard's brief suborbital flight signaled that the United States was still a contender. As the third Mercury spacecraft to launch on a Redstone rocket, the mission's official name was Mercury-Redstone 3.

The design of the Mercury spacecraft was a direct result of NASA's hastened pace to send humans to space after the Soviet Sputnik launch in 1957. Instead of taking the time to construct and test a spaceplane with wings and landing gear—a design familiar to sci-fi fans—

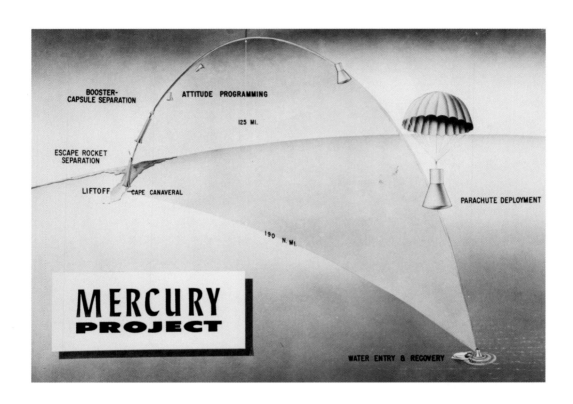

BOOSTER-CAPSULE SEPARATION   ATTITUDE PROGRAMMING

125 MI.

ESCAPE ROCKET SEPARATION

LIFTOFF   CAPE CANAVERAL

190 N. MI.

PARACHUTE DEPLOYMENT

MERCURY
PROJECT

WATER ENTRY & RECOVERY

NASA adapted ballistic missiles and their reentry vehicles, which were already under development. The physics of atmospheric reentry determined the Mercury capsule's bell-like shape. Research on warheads had already discovered that, at high speeds, streamlined objects like airplanes vaporize in the heat caused by friction with the atmosphere on reentry. Wide, rounded shapes moving at hypersonic speeds, however, create a shock wave that deflects superheated air away from the vehicle. Heat shielding absorbs most of the remaining heat, leaving the capsule cabin at a temperate degree.

In January 1959, NASA awarded McDonnell Aircraft Corporation in St. Louis, Missouri, the contract to develop,

> "It's a very sobering feeling to be up in space and realize that one's safety factor was determined by the lowest bidder on a government contract."
>
> —Alan Shepard, first American in space

test, and build the Mercury spacecraft. It fabricated the cone-shaped capsule out of titanium and beryllium, lightweight but strong materials. For safety, the spacecraft could be operated through automatic or manual control. Both the cabin and the Mercury space suits had a 100 percent oxygen environment. Each capsule was also equipped with a contoured couch, to transfer bodily loads during the flight's intense acceleration and deceleration.

As McDonnell worked to make a craft to carry the first U.S. space traveler, NASA set out to find that person. The task group initially intended to open up a general application to all men with a "willingness to accept hazards" and the capacity to handle stress. They thought that test pilots, submarine captains, and Arctic explorers would be ideal. Eisenhower, however, limited the application pool to U.S. military test pilots, who were already available for service. Of more than 100 qualified test pilots, seven were selected, on April 9, 1959, introduced as the Mercury astronauts. Each named his own capsule, including the number "7" in honor of the size of the group.

In the five minutes Alan Shepard spent in microgravity, he proved the Mercury capsule pilotable, that weightlessness had little negative effect on the human body (at least for brief periods), and that NASA's system to launch and track spacecraft was viable. Not until John Glenn and the third crewed Mercury mission would an American orbit the globe as Gagarin had. But Shepard's brief trip demonstrated that U.S. astronauts could fly in space. •

The NASA Art Program

NASA administrator James Webb created the NASA Art Program after seeing this portrait of Alan Shepard by Bruce Stevenson in 1961. He believed that art could capture the spirit of space exploration in a way that photos could not.

When NASA administrator James Webb first saw artist Bruce Stevenson's portrait of astronaut Alan Shepard, it inspired him. The portrait captured something special that no camera, newspaper article, or report could record. In 1962, Webb penned a memo calling for the creation of an art program for the space agency. "Important events," he later explained, "can be interpreted by artists to give a unique insight into significant aspects of our history-making advances into space." Since its creation in the early 1960s, the NASA Art Program has assisted hundreds of artists, musicians, poets, and even a fashion designer, in interpreting the exploration of outer space and offering diverse perspectives on the American space program.

To carry out Webb's vision, James Dean—an artist in NASA's Public Affairs Office—teamed up with H. Lester Cooke, curator of paintings at the National Gallery of Art in Washington, D.C. Notable American artists— from illustrator Norman Rockwell to abstract expressionist Robert Rauschenberg—traveled to NASA facilities to observe both historic missions and the day-to-day work of the space program. Artists were present on the ground, aboard recovery ships, and in the clean rooms, reproducing man and machine as they prepared for their missions from the last Mercury mission through Gemini and Apollo. Cooke felt that it was the "emotional impact, interpretation, and hidden significance of these events which lie within the scope of the artist's vision." Though the average honorarium was only $800, artists enthusiastically participated in the program.

By the end of the Apollo Project, the NASA Art Program yielded nearly 3,000 pieces. Much of this work is now part of the Smithsonian National Air and Space Museum's collection. From small human moments on the ground to awe-inspiring rocket launches, the art of Apollo brings space exploration to a human scale. As Cooke wrote, "I hope that future generations will realize that we have not only scientists and engineers capable of shaping the destiny of our age, but also artists worthy to keep them company."

Alan B Shepard Jr
Painted by
Bruce Stevenson

7 John Glenn's Ansco Camera

Date: 1962
Manufacturer: Minolta
Origin: Japan and the United States
Materials: Metal, glass, quartz, plastic, Velcro
Dimensions: $5^{5}/_{16}$ by $2^{15}/_{16}$ by $9^{5}/_{8}$ inches

Mercury astronaut John Glenn purchased an Ansco Autoset camera at a drug store in the winter of 1962. Although of humble origin, it was the tool Glenn used to capture the first human-shot, color, still photographs from space.

Initially, photography was not part of Glenn's orbital mission. The camera designated for his flight was configured for scientific studies, not mission documentation, and NASA treated human interest photography as a distraction from the engineering goals of Project Mercury. Handheld cameras were not an option on the first American human spaceflight, as Alan Shepard's *Freedom 7* capsule was not even outfitted with a pilot's window. Although NASA added a trapezoidal window to Gus Grissom's *Liberty Bell 7,* this second piloted Mercury mission also did not include photography. But Glenn believed sharing the adventure of spaceflight with the world was essential, and that photographs "would help translate an astronaut's experience for anyone who saw them." He pleaded his case to Robert Gilruth, director of NASA's Manned Spaceflight Center (later Johnson Space Center) in Houston, who eventually consented.

Following a pre-mission haircut in Cocoa Beach, Florida, Glenn stopped into a nearby drug store where he spotted a camera. Picking it up, he noted that it had automatic exposure settings. This meant Glenn would not have to adjust the camera, freeing up precious time and attention during the brief mission. In addition to the camera's then state-of-the-art features, it had a straightforward and user-friendly design. He purchased

"I don't know what you could say about a day in which you have seen four beautiful sunsets."

—John Glenn, after his Friendship 7 flight

the camera for $45 and brought it back to NASA.

Because Glenn would be flying in a space suit, with bulky gloves and a fishbowl-like helmet, the camera had to be modified. Roland "Red" Williams, an RCA contractor, first flipped the camera upside down to align his improvised pistol grip handle controls with the camera's advance dial and exposure button. The handle made it possible for Glenn to hold the camera and trigger an exposure with one hand. Williams then added a replacement Polaroid eyepiece to the new "top" of the camera, to allow Glenn to photograph Earth unhindered by his helmet.

On February 20, 1962, John Glenn rode a massive Atlas rocket into Earth orbit with the Ansco and a Leica camera in tow. He would become the first American to orbit Earth, following the suborbital flights of his fellow Mercury astronauts. Glenn used the Ansco for point-and-shoot daytime or horizon photography, while the Leica was outfitted with a spectrographic lens for ultraviolet images of the constellation Orion. In microgravity, the Ansco camera was a success, with Glenn later recalling, "When I needed both hands, I just let go of the camera, and it floated there in front of me."

Although Glenn's photographs circulated to publications around the world, they hardly achieved the iconic status of later Apollo astronaut photography. It took years before NASA prioritized the public dissemination of images from space. Because NASA officials saw photography as a means of engineering documentation and scientific research, they hesitated to make it a significant part of early flight plans. •

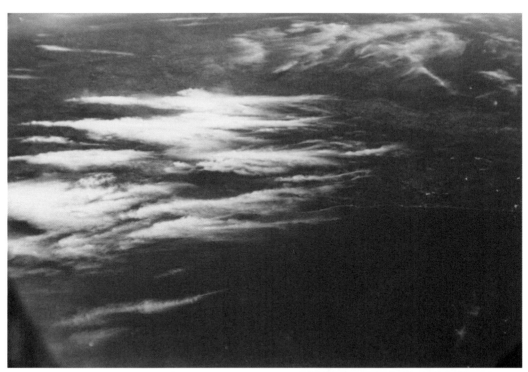

New Challenges

Introduction

"Not because they are easy, but because they are hard . . ."

Less than a decade after President Kennedy proposed Project Apollo in 1961, the United States landed the first crewed spacecraft on the moon. This ambitious journey required a warlike mobilization, drawing on a workforce in the hundreds of thousands, with a budget that outstripped all previous civilian scientific and technological programs by orders of magnitude, and overcoming dozens of new engineering challenges.

On September 12, 1962, before an audience of 40,000 people gathered under a bright Texan sun, Kennedy rallied support for lunar exploration in a now historic speech at Rice University. He asked, "But why, some say, the moon? Why choose this as our goal?" The president added his own line, jotted down between the margins of the printed speech, to appeal to the hometown crowd: "Why does Rice play Texas?"

Then Kennedy made the case for American investment in space exploration to thundering applause: "We choose to go to the moon in this

But why, some say, the moon? Why choose this as our goal? And they may as well ask: why climb the highest mountain? Why 35 years ago *Why does Rice play Texas* fly the Atlantic? We choose to go to the moon in this decade, not because that will be easy, but because it will be hard -- because that goal will serve to organize and measure the best of our energies and skills -- because that challenge is one we are willing to accept, one we are unwilling to postpone, and one we intend to win.

decade and do the other things, not because they are <u>easy</u>, but because they are <u>hard</u>, because that goal will serve to organize and measure the best of our energies and skills, because that challenge is one that we are willing to accept, one we are unwilling to postpone, and one which we intend to win, and the others, too."

As the president predicted, the U.S. space program did have to overcome a number of difficulties and challenges in order to reach the moon. New technologies, new capabilities, new managerial organization, and new training techniques all came together to ensure the astronauts' safety on bold new missions beyond our planet and to the lunar surface. •

8 Gemini 7 Capsule

Date: 1965
Manufacturer: McDonnell Aircraft Corporation
Origin: St. Louis, Missouri
Materials: Titanium, beryllium alloy, Rene 41 nickel-steel alloy, silicone elastomer heat shield
Dimensions: 10 feet 10 inches by 7 feet 5 inches

Project Mercury demonstrated that American technology could safely send humans to space and return them to Earth. Project Gemini demonstrated that NASA had the capabilities necessary for lunar exploration. Over the course of 10 missions, between 1965 and 1966, American astronauts tested extra-vehicular activity (or "spacewalks"), rendezvous and docking, and long-duration spaceflight. A two-seated capsule (opposite) carried astronauts Frank Borman and James "Jim" Lovell on a record-setting two-week mission, during which they participated in the first rendezvous in orbit and performed a series of biomedical experiments, paving the way for future moon missions.

When Gemini 7 launched on December 4, 1965, no one knew for sure how microgravity would affect the human body over the length of an Apollo mission. Borman and Lovell conducted 20 experiments, many related to their own cardiovascular, muscular, and digestive systems. They lived on Houston time, sleeping during the same 10-hour period and synchronizing meals with a specific flight controller called the capsule communicator, or CAPCOM. Two full weeks of food, logbooks, experimental equipment, personal items, trash, and even fecal waste were stored inside their small capsule. Before the flight, the crew had rehearsed where every instrument would go and where every item—no matter how small—would be stowed. Nevertheless, they still managed to lose one of their toothbrushes mid-mission.

Borman and Lovell wore specially developed pressure suits, which, although bulky, weighed considerably less than previous garments. These suits came equipped with flexible zippered hoods instead of rigid helmets. Once in orbit, the men removed their hoods and gloves. Forty-eight hours into the mission, the astronauts took alternating turns in the capsule without wearing their cumbersome suits. Lovell went first. It took him almost an hour to squeeze out of his suit, but once he did, he found the cabin environment quite comfortable. While Lovell enjoyed the freedom of being suit-less, Borman's suit could not keep him cool. It took eight days of arguing with ground control before NASA gave permission for both astronauts to be out of the suits simultaneously.

A month before launch, Gemini 7 received an additional mission objective—complete the first rendezvous in orbit. On October 25, 1965, NASA had planned a same-day launch of Gemini 6 and a crewless craft called the Agena, to test rendezvous and docking. But after the Agena exploded over the Atlantic, two McDonnell officials proposed switching the planned order of the missions. The Gemini 6 craft was set aside, allowing Gemini 7 to launch as planned. After Borman and Lovell were in orbit, the pad was quickly cleared, and Gemini 6—

redesignated Gemini 6-A—was prepped for launch. On December 15—an unprecedented 11 days after Borman and Lovell had taken off—NASA launched astronauts Walter Schirra and Thomas Stafford. The crew of Gemini 6-A quickly located Gemini 7, and the crafts maintained a distance between a foot and 200 feet apart for hours before separating.

The Gemini 7 mission was exhausting and at times tedious, and the astronauts brought books along for entertainment during their mission. Borman had Mark Twain's *Roughing It,* while Lovell brought along *Drums Along the Mohawk,* by Walter D. Edmonds. When they finally splashed down in the Atlantic Ocean on December 18, 1965, both astronauts were tired but physically fit, proving that astronauts could fly to the moon and back without risking their health. •

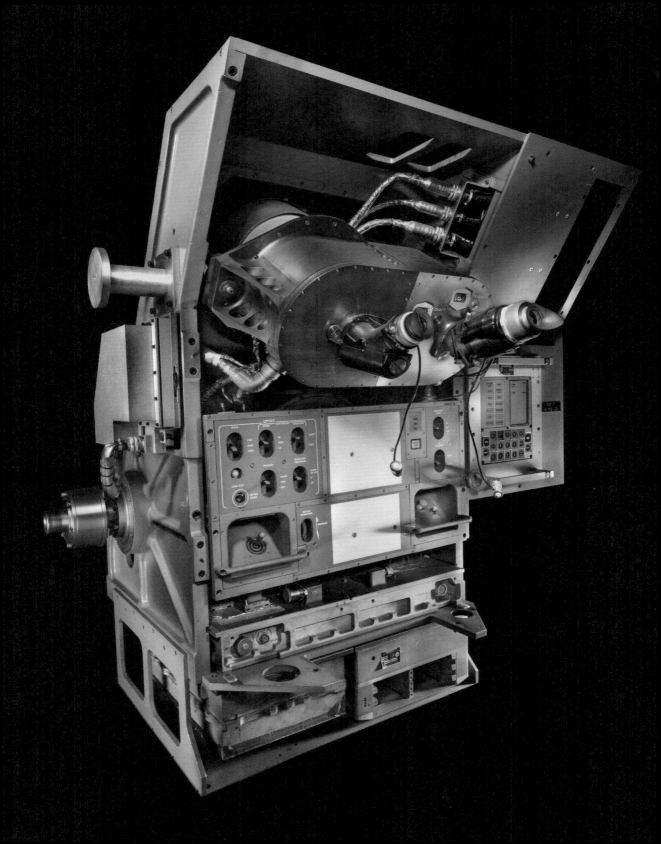

9 Apollo Guidance Computer

Date: Mid-1960s
Manufacturer: Raytheon;
MIT Instrumentation Laboratory
Origin: Cambridge and Waltham,
Massachusetts
Materials: Aluminum, steel, various
metals, plastics, and glass
Dimensions: 3 feet 4 inches by
3 feet by 3 feet 10 inches

It could be called the brains of the Apollo spacecraft. Awarded on a sole source basis to the Massachusetts Institute of Technology (MIT) in August 1961, less than 10 weeks after President Kennedy's announcement of the lunar landing goal, the Apollo Guidance Computer (AGC) was the only major Apollo contract performed by a university.

NASA was confident in MIT's technical expertise to develop the inertial guidance system capable of navigating a spacecraft to the moon and back. But personal relationships between Charles Stark Draper, the MIT Instrumentation Laboratory director, and NASA administrator James Webb mattered most. (Webb worked at Sperry Gyroscope when Draper developed the innovative Mark 14 gunsight used to defend naval ships during World War II.) When Webb asked Draper how he knew the AGC would work, the 60-year-old engineer responded by volunteering to personally fly on the first Apollo lunar mission, promptly submitting his application to NASA's astronaut program.

Draper proposed the AGC's modest specifications: It would weigh less than 100 pounds, take up no more than a single cubic foot of space, and consume less than 100 watts of power. He intended to use a highly reliable magnetic core memory, common in both commercial and military systems of that era, when Eldon Hall, the computer's chief hardware engineer, made a radical recommendation: to use integrated circuits from a start-up company, Fairchild Semiconductor, to improve computational speed while maintaining the computer's size and weight. Ultimately over a million chips of this new and unproven technology were produced for the Apollo program alone.

Initially envisioned as a guidance, navigation, and control system for the Apollo command module, the AGC relied on a highly precise inertial guidance platform that used gyroscopes and accelerometers to measure the spacecraft's position, velocity, and acceleration. To account for drift in the platform's accuracy, the precise location in space could be updated using star sightings conducted by the astronauts themselves, via sextant and telescope. A display and keyboard, known simply by the acronym DSKY, provided the primary interface between human and machine. Using a limited architecture of nouns and verbs, the data informed the astronauts about critical mission events.

When MIT proposed the AGC in 1961, the word "software" was not yet invented. By 1966, a majority of the MIT engineers were working on software rather than hardware. Modern comparisons of the AGC's limited processing speed and minimal memory to the vastly more powerful capability carried in present-day smartphones miss the point. Although the AGC had severe limitations relative to today's computers, its design was ingeniously robust and efficient. Software development occurred using punch cards and required overnight runs on MIT's mainframe computer. A hybrid simulator consisting of both analog and digital computers was used to test the AGC hardware and software in real time with humans in the control loop.

With names like Colossus and Luminary, Apollo's software was written in assembly language instructions, and could be fully comprehended by the individual engineers who wrote it. When Apollo 14's lunar landing was

seriously threatened by a faulty abort switch, 27-year-old engineer Don Eyles devised a workaround, tested it on the hybrid simulator, and sent it to Mission Control. There it was read up to astronauts Alan Shepard and Ed Mitchell, who manually entered it using the DSKY. Developed in less than two hours, this masterful ingenuity saved the lunar landing mission, demonstrating the resilience of the Apollo Guidance Computer and the human scale of its elegant software.

The AGC performed flawlessly throughout each of the Apollo mis-sions without even a single hardware failure. Although each Apollo commander would ultimately take over manual control in the final lunar landing phase, their inputs were routed through the computer's digital autopilot, which controlled the descent engine and attitude control system. As MIT's program manager Dave Hoag would later state, "in an incredible and audacious task, the landing of men on the moon, the guidance equipment for the mission was created out of primitive principles, prolific imagination, and a lot of hard work." •

Margaret Hamilton, Lead Apollo Flight Software Designer

"Software engineering" was not a term in use when Margaret Hamilton began to program computers. Born in Indiana in 1936, Hamilton graduated from Earlham College in 1958 and took a job programming computers for the Massachusetts Institute of Technology (MIT) two years later. At MIT Hamilton began a career-long interest in fixing programming errors. In those early days of programming, Hamilton and her peers learned engineering and troubleshooting on the job, finding creative ways to assess their work. They could sometimes tell if their software was running smoothly by the background noises the huge computers made.

In 1963, as Hamilton was preparing to enter graduate school at Brandeis University for a degree in abstract mathematics, MIT earned a contract from NASA to design the guidance and navigation computer (AGC) for the Apollo spacecraft. Not wanting to miss the opportunity, Hamilton called the program office to set up interviews with two project managers. They both offered her a job on the spot. She suggested they should flip a coin to decide which team would take her on. Within a few years, Hamilton would become director of the Software Engineering Division at the MIT Instrumentation Lab, and one of the lead minds behind the AGC.

In designing the software for the Apollo Guidance Computer, Hamilton and her team had to create a new software system to navigate and control the Apollo spacecraft on missions to the moon. "There was no choice but to be pioneers . . . When answers could not be found, we had to invent them," she later observed. The team was full of "fearless 20-something-year-olds" who had the freedom, and the pressure, to tackle the challenges of space navigation.

Over the course of the Apollo and Skylab program, while Hamilton's software was in use, there was never a major failure. Hamilton's daughter, Lauren, foretold one of the worst mistakes. While playing with a DSKY unit in Hamilton's office when she was four years old, Lauren entered the code for a prelaunch program P01 while the simulator was in midflight, trig-

gering a major error. In response, Hamilton suggested a line of code that would prevent that event, but was informed by NASA that no astronaut would ever make such a mistake.

During Apollo 8, Jim Lovell accidentally wiped out the command and service module's navigation data, creating the same situation that Hamilton's daughter had made. But because of the computer's robust design, Hamilton and her team were able to find a way to correct the problem from the ground within hours, and to see the mission to a successful completion.

Hamilton later worked with NASA on the development of the space shuttle software. She also founded two companies specializing in designing reliable and trustworthy software, and was awarded the Presidential Medal of Freedom in 2016 for her work on Project Apollo. Always one of the few women in the room, Hamilton stands out among the individuals who made the Apollo program the success it was, and helped usher computing into outer space.

10 Apollo Mission Simulators

Date: Mid-1960s
Manufacturer: Link Aviation, a division of General Precision
Origin: Binghamton, New York
Materials: Steel and various metals, plastics, glass optics and windows
Dimensions: Control console: 8 feet 1 inch by 5 feet by 3 feet 11 inches

Apollo 11 astronaut Michael Collins described simulation as the "heart and soul of NASA." Fellow astronaut John Young was less charitable, describing the odd-shaped Apollo Mission Simulator as a "great train wreck."

Designed and built by Link Aviation in Binghamton, New York, the Apollo Mission Simulator and the Lunar Mission Simulator were at the core of NASA's program for training—not only for the Apollo astronauts but also for the entire Mission Control team. It schooled them in the intricate procedures necessary to successfully execute a lunar landing mission.

The Apollo simulators pushed the state of the art in simulator technology, achieving a high degree of fidelity and realism, including the visual and audio cues that astronauts would experience during a flight to the moon.

Precise replication of the spacecraft instrument panels and cockpit controls was essential. Embedded in the software that drove the Apollo simulators were the mathematical equations of motion governing a flight to the moon. Supported by room-size analog and digital computers, every dynamic phase of the Apollo missions could be synthetically flown in real time with six degrees of freedom. That meant moving forward and backward, up and down, left and right, while rotating.

The assemblage of oddly shaped geometries surrounding the spacecraft itself were the optical systems developed by Farrand Optical in the Bronx,

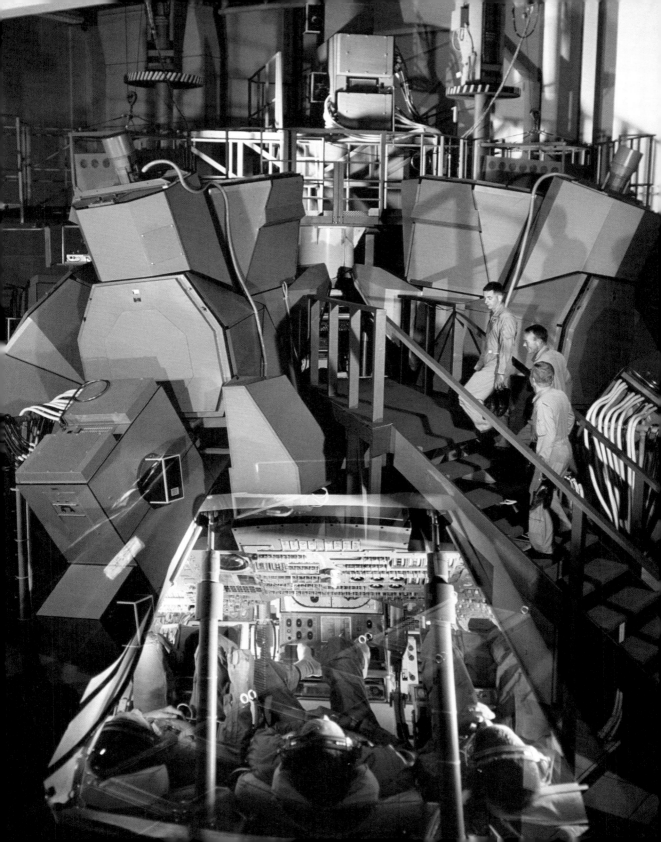

New York, to display high-resolution images on each of the spacecraft windows. In this way, the astronauts could practice star sightings using Apollo's sextant and telescope, critical for updating the spacecraft's inertial guidance system.

When the simulators first arrived at NASA in 1966, Link's engineers worked diligently to assure that they identically matched the rapidly changing spacecraft configuration. Soon thereafter

NASA established a control board to minimize changes in both hardware and software, stabilizing the configuration of both the Apollo spacecraft and their simulators.

Simulator supervisors (affectionately known as "Sim Sups") and their teams of instructors developed a clever series of challenging yet believable malfunctions to challenge Apollo flight crews to respond correctly in real-time situations. Integrated mission simulations were frequently conducted with both Apollo spacecraft simulators networked to NASA's Mission Control center. This highly realistic training was aimed at both the astronauts who would fly the missions and the flight controllers who would monitor spacecraft telemetry and assure that mission operations were conducted safely.

By 1968, the Apollo simulators became trusted and reliable tools. Because they could so closely replicate spacecraft functions, the Apollo simulators were used to develop the complex procedures necessary to execute increasingly challenging missions. During Apollo's first flight, frustrated commander Walter "Wally" Schirra belligerently urged Mission Control to take an unplanned procedure "over to the simulator, run it through, and if it wrings out, we may try it."

Apollo astronauts spent hundreds of hours training in these simulators in the months leading up to their missions. During each of the lunar missions, the astronauts inevitably compared the real experience of flying to the moon to the virtual experience that they had encountered during training. The phrase "just like the simulator" can be found in the transcripts from every Apollo mission.

Perhaps most memorably, the mission simulators helped save the flight crew of Apollo 13 after an explosion disabled all major spacecraft functions. On the ground, as teams of astronauts, simulator instructors, and flight controllers developed the intricate procedures to operate the crippled spacecraft, the Apollo Mission Simulators worked around the clock to validate each and every corrective action. These included the complex procedures to power up the dormant Apollo command module just prior to reentry into Earth's atmosphere, a scenario that had never been contemplated by even the most devious simulation supervisors. The result was the safe return of Apollo 13 back to Earth, what some have called NASA's "finest hour." •

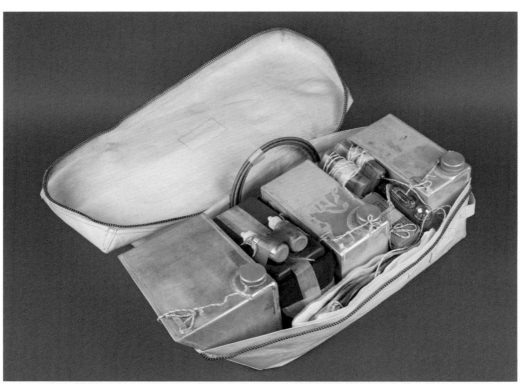

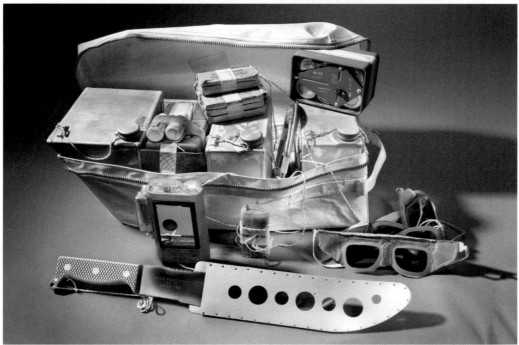

11 Survival Kit, Apollo 11

Date: Manufactured in 1968, flown in 1969
Manufacturer: B. Welson & Co.
Origin: Hartford, Connecticut
Materials: Beta cloth, brass, steel, plastic, glass, nylon, foam, Velcro
Dimensions: 1 foot 9½ inches by 1 foot by 1 foot 7½ inches

The blunt body of the command module (CM) kept Apollo crews safe from intense frictional heat during reentry, but it limited precise landings. The CM's trajectory as it pierced the atmosphere was the main determinant of where it would splash down in the ocean. NASA designed contingency plans in case the capsule landed a great distance from the U.S. Navy vessels stationed for recovery, or in a foreign country. The survival kit from the Apollo 11 mission (opposite) was luckily never used. The CM *Columbia* landed without mishap in the Pacific Ocean just 12 nautical miles from their recovery ship, the U.S.S. *Hornet*.

The kit was equipped with an emergency radio beacon with replacement batteries; three water jugs that could be filled from the capsule's water supply or with seawater run through the included desalination kit; a pair of multifunctional survival lights complete with compass; fishing line; water purification tablets; a fire starter; three pairs of sunglasses; two bottles of sunscreen; and a machete.

The astronauts rehearsed splashdowns over and over, as they did every aspect of their mission. This training involved a simple exit from the spacecraft in water, the expected landing environment. Even in calm seas, climbing out of the CM could be dangerous. Astronauts practiced exiting their ships first in controlled pools, and then in the open water of the Gulf of Mexico. If everything went according to plan, recovery swimmers deployed from helicopters would be there to assist

" . . . as in the case of so much astronaut training, the information has never really been needed, but it . . . was prudent to . . . prepare people for as many variations . . . as possible."

—Michael Collins,
Carrying the Fire

astronauts after splashdown. But in the event that the capsule landed outside of the recovery area, NASA supplied each craft with a three-person inflatable raft along with a survival kit, to provide protection for up to 48 hours in open water.

NASA also prepared the astronauts for the less likely event that their capsules crash-landed on solid ground. Because this would most likely occur in a tropical rain forest or desert, training took place around the Panama Canal and on Stead Air Force Base in Reno, Nevada. After classroom instruction on survival, NASA left the astronauts in the wilderness for several days with a trainer, their undergarments, and the supplies planned for their capsule. This exercise also

tested the effectiveness of the survival kit, prompting the development of additional rescue strategies, including water drops from search planes.

In the end, all Apollo spacecraft landed no more than a few miles from their target zones. As astronaut Michael Collins noted, "Thus, as in the case of so much astronaut training, the information has never really been needed, but it nonetheless was prudent to try to prepare people for as many variations upon the expected theme as possible." •

12 Robert Foster's McDonnell Jacket

Date: 1960s
Manufacturer: Unknown
Origin: United States
Materials: Cotton/poly fabric, embroidery thread, metal zipper, plastic buttons
Dimensions: 2 feet 2 inches by 5 feet 6 inches

Hundreds of thousands of people worked to make the lunar landings a reality. President John F. Kennedy's 1961 call to send humans to the moon and return them safely back to Earth within the short period of a decade required a mass mobilization of resources, including an expanded workforce. NASA determined the requirements of a new technology and a timetable for its completion, and then put the project out to bid. The space agency focused on managing and unifying what became many different programs and facilities spread across the country.

While NASA grew from 10,000 employees in 1960 to 36,000 by 1966, the increase in contractor employees swelled by a factor of 10. In 1960, 36,500 people from private industry, research institutions, and universities worked on the American space program. By 1965, that number reached 376,700. Many wore uniforms, like the jacket (see page 81) that belonged to Robert Lee Foster. An engineer at the McDonnell Aircraft Corporation, Foster was one of the hundreds of thousands of contract employees whose efforts propelled America into space.

Robert "Bob" Foster was born on February 7, 1922, in Jacksonville, Illinois. In 1942, he left Washington University in St. Louis to join the Army, rising to the rank of captain in the Army Corps of Engineers before leaving in 1950. He received a scholarship to the Georgia Institute of Technology that same year and graduated in 1952 with a bachelor's degree in electrical engineering. Immediately after graduation, the McDonnell Aircraft Corporation hired him for their Airplane Engineering Division Design Department. When NASA awarded McDonnell the Mercury spacecraft contract in 1958, the company assigned Foster to the design team. In 1959, Foster moved to Florida with his wife, Antoinette ("Toni"), and their three children, to become the chief electrical engineer for the Mercury program and then, eventually, operations manager for Project Gemini. McDonnell, which merged with the Douglas Aircraft Company to create McDonnell Douglas in 1967, was the prime contractor for both the Mercury and Gemini spacecraft, as well as the Saturn-IVB stage rockets.

Bob Foster and his family were not the only contractors who relocated to Florida during the space age. As more and more of the American space program centered its operations at Cape Canaveral in the late 1950s and early

1960s, the area's population increased tenfold. Housing developments spread across the region, scores of new schools opened, and the world turned its eye to Florida's east coast. Toni Foster, in her 1961 Christmas letter to family, said of her new home, "Cocoa Beach is a study of contrasts . . . It is really just a sleepy

little southern town which has suddenly found itself famous." While she taught elementary school and did everyday things, her husband's work with NASA, and his familiarity with the astronauts, could make their life anything but normal. In the same Christmas letter, she recounts being out to dinner with her family when Mercury astronauts Scott Carpenter and John Glenn stopped by the table to say hello. It took, she shared, nearly an hour to leave the restaurant as reporters surrounded her family, trying to find out who they were, given that they knew some of the most famous people in the world on a first-name basis. •

The Assembly

Introduction

"The best ship to come down the line . . ."

The lunar orbit rendezvous approach to the moon suggested a three-part spacecraft: command module (CM), service module (SM), and lunar module (LM). A Saturn V rocket would send all three on their lunar trajectory, acting together as one vehicle. Once the astronauts reached lunar orbit, the lunar module would separate from the command and service modules and land on the moon's surface. After moonwalks were complete, the astronauts would reenter the LM and lift off in the ascent stage, meeting the CM in orbit. The crew would then plunge through Earth's atmosphere and splash down in the Pacific Ocean aboard the blunt-body CM.

Apollo astronauts grew fond of the spacecraft, and for good reason. The Apollo assembly did what had never been done before: safely ferried astronauts to and from the moon. "When we got back in that command module, we were home," remembers Gene Cernan, commander of Apollo 17, on his return from the lunar surface.

At the end of the Apollo 11 mission in July 1969, once safely quarantined aboard the aircraft carrier rescue vessel

A NASA artist's concept illustration shows the Apollo spacecraft in launch configuration, including a stowed lunar module and the launch escape system, which would carry the astronauts to safety in the event of an accident during launch.

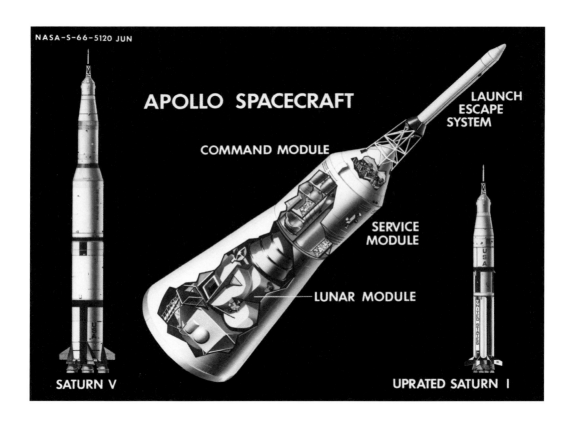

NASA-S-66-5120 JUN

APOLLO SPACECRAFT

LAUNCH ESCAPE SYSTEM

COMMAND MODULE

SERVICE MODULE

LUNAR MODULE

SATURN V

UPRATED SATURN I

U.S.S. *Hornet* near the splashdown site in the Pacific Ocean, astronaut Mike Collins climbed back into the CM *Columbia* one last time. With a pen, he wrote a note on an inside panel, above the sextant port: "The best ship to come down the line. God Bless Her. Michael Collins, CMP."

It took thousands of people working across the country to produce the major components for Project Apollo. The stories behind the development of the Apollo assembly underscore the complexity and precision required to send humans to the moon. •

13 Saturn V Instrument Unit

Date: ca 1970
Manufacturer: Federal Systems Division, IBM
Origin: Huntsville, Alabama
Materials: Aluminum electronic parts
Dimensions: 36 inches by 21 feet 8³/₈ inches

One of the first and most challenging steps to putting humans on the moon was breaking the chains of Earth's gravity. To lift the unprecedented heavy payload of three space vehicles, NASA had to create an unprecedented rocket. The Saturn V was the culmination of years of work and decades of theorizing. The National Air and Space Museum has stewardship of three complete Saturn Vs, though only segments are small enough to fit in the halls of the museum: like the Saturn V Instrument Unit (Saturn V IU). This large, ring-shaped device is the computerized brain of the tower-

ing rocket that helped guarantee that Apollo astronauts reached the moon.

The Saturn V is a multistage vehicle, standing 363 feet tall when fully assembled. It consists of three separate stages that fire in sequence to reach orbit. Each stage is its own separately developed and constructed rocket: the first stage, S-IC; the second stage, S-II; and the third stage, S-IVB. Each rocket contains two tanks, one filled with liquid oxygen (LOX) and the other with either RP-1 (a highly refined form of kerosene) or liquid hydrogen (LH2), depending on the stage. When the fuel mixed with the oxygen and ignited, it caused a continuous reaction that propelled the rocket at immense speeds. During a launch, the first stage consumed over 300,000 gallons of LOX and 200,000 gallons of RP-1 in just two and a half minutes, accelerating the craft to around 6,000 miles an hour. The first stage then fell away, landing in the Atlantic Ocean. At this point, the second-stage rocket fired and propelled the craft nearly to orbit, at an altitude of 114 miles, in six minutes.

The third stage then took over, for about two and a half minutes, to achieve an orbital altitude of 118 miles and a speed of more than 17,500 miles an hour. The Instrument Unit had to withstand forces of the firings of the three stages while guiding the Saturn V on its trajectory.

The IBM Corporation, the prime contractor, and General Dynamics, which built the honeycomb structure, managed this feat by building the walls of the ring out of an aluminum honeycomb. This structure bore the entire force of the Saturn V launches in a little less than an inch of material. Once in Earth orbit, the Instrument Unit's computer checked all systems and made minor adjustments. After determining that everything was working, the computer commanded the third stage to restart, and give the Apollo craft the final push toward the moon. Once on its way to the lunar target, the third stage and the attached Instrument Unit separated itself from the payload.

The Instrument Unit served a vital role at the initial stage of the flight. It tracked the rocket's course, controlled maneuvering and separation sequences, and received commands from ground control as well as, if necessary, the command module. During the first stage of launch, the Saturn V followed a programmed series of maneuvers. The four outer F-1 engines that powered the Saturn V were mounted on gimbals, which allowed the engines to steer the craft as it ascended off the launchpad. The computer recorded any deviations from the programmed course but waited to make any adjustments, as any correction during this phase risked putting undue stress on the rocket and potentially breaking it apart in midair. The IU sent orders to each stage to separate at a certain point, detonating charges that severed their connections, and activating small rockets that pushed the spent stage away from the rest of the spacecraft. It interfaced with the command module computer and ground control during checkouts as the third stage and the Apollo craft orbited Earth before heading to the moon. Finally, the IU put

the S-IVB on a solar orbit or, in later missions, crashed it into the moon itself as part of seismic experiments.

The Instrument Unit's computer, officially the Launch Vehicle Digital Computer, differed in fundamental ways from the Apollo Guidance Computer (AGC), although each was a significant technical feat. The AGC had no inherent redundancy, but rather relied on commands from Mission Control in Houston if anything went wrong with the command module's computer, and on an Abort Guidance System on the lunar module if the LM guidance computer failed. The Instrument Unit computer, on the other hand, achieved reliability through redundancy. IBM replicated every circuit in triplicate. If the three circuits did not agree during an operation, a voting circuit picked the majority command, which allowed for potential failures in individual circuits. Of the 32 Saturn rockets launched, there were never any failures—an unheard-of statistic in early rocketry. •

Wernher von Braun and the Development of Rocketry

No one symbolizes the rocket's two-sided Janus face better than Wernher von Braun. As technical director of the Nazi V-2 ballistic missile project, he made it possible to drop a warhead on a distant city in five minutes. And as director of the NASA Marshall Space Flight Center, he managed the coast-to-coast team that designed, built, and delivered the gigantic Saturn V rocket—the one that sent Apollo astronauts to the moon.

Born into the Prussian nobility in 1912, Baron von Braun became infatuated with spaceflight as a teenager. He decided to pursue liquid-fuel rocketry, which pioneering spaceflight theorists showed could accelerate a vehicle to unheard-of velocities. Obsessed with the idea of leading a moon expedition, he joined a Berlin rocket club while in university there.

In late 1932, as Germany descended into political chaos, von Braun pursued a secret doctoral dissertation on liquid-propellant rocket development, funded by the army. Shortly after he began, Adolf Hitler established a totalitarian dictatorship. Von Braun, raised in a right-wing nationalist household, was little bothered and soon saw the benefit of Nazi rearmament money as his small project grew into a supersecret rocket development center on the Baltic at Peenemünde. With the start of World War II in 1939, pressure increased to produce an operational weapon. After much delay, Germany finally launched the V-2 against Allied cities in late 1944. The missile was assembled underground using concentration-camp labor, where the brutal conditions caused more deaths than were ever exacted by missile impacts. Von Braun, who had somewhat reluctantly become a party member and SS officer to further his career, was implicated in that criminal enterprise.

But no reckoning came at war's end, as the United States wanted to master V-2 technology and develop guided missiles. In El Paso, Texas, and then Huntsville, Alabama, von Braun led a group of more than a hundred Germans working on U.S. Army missile projects. Still obsessed with space travel, he used his spare time to sell it to a still skeptical public. In 1952, he had a breakthrough when his articles in Collier's magazine reached a mass audience, leading to television stardom on Walt Disney's program. After the Soviet Sputnik triumph in fall 1957, his team orbited the first U.S. satellite, Explorer 1. Von Braun's Huntsville group was soon diverted from nuclear-armed ballistic missiles to a big space booster, Saturn. In 1959, President Eisenhower directed that his team, now numbering several thousand Americans, be transferred to the new NASA.

For Apollo, von Braun's role was to be the maestro of a huge project to develop the Saturn I, IB, and V. The enormous scale required aerospace companies to develop and manufacture giant rocket stages at facilities in California and Louisiana. Although von Braun did not design the launch vehicles, he was their indispensable engineering manager, demonstrating his exceptional talent for assembling and leading a large team to develop exotic technologies. He will always be remembered for his seminal contributions to rocketry and spaceflight, but also for the moral compromises he made to further his career in the Third Reich.

14 Lunar Module 2

Date: Late 1960s
Manufacturer: Grumman Aircraft Engineering Corporation
Origin: Bethpage, New York
Materials: Aluminum, titanium, aluminized Mylar, and aluminized Kapton blankets
Dimensions: 21 feet 5½ inches by 21 feet 5½ inches

The lunar module (LM), with its spindly legs and boxy body, may appear ill equipped to take flight, let alone fly in the hazardous conditions of outer space. But this spiderlike spacecraft landed astronauts on the moon and returned them safely to lunar orbit.

Grumman Aircraft Engineering Corporation, in the Long Island, New York town of Bethpage, was known for designing aircraft for the U.S. Navy—ones that could tolerate hard landings on aircraft carriers. This expertise helped the company win the contract to develop and build a spacecraft to land on an unfamiliar celestial body with just one-sixth of Earth's gravity. Not only did the extremely lightweight lunar modules need to land safely, but also they had to withstand the vacuum of space and allow astronauts to exit and enter the craft multiple times.

The vehicle was made up of two stages: the upper ascent stage and the lower descent stage. The upper stage contained the pressurized crew compartment, equipment area, and ascent rocket engine, and the lower stage housed the descent engine and landing gear. After landing, the descent stage would remain on the moon while the ascent stage ferried the crew to reunite with the command module in orbit.

All of the lunar modules have unique appearances; each is essentially hand-crafted. Engineers taped and stapled on the multilayered blankets of Mylar and Kapton. They hand-crinkled each of the layers, ensuring that there would be gaps of air that could further insulate the spacecraft. Outfitted with its own guidance and navigation, life support, communications, and instrumentation, the lunar module needed to ferry two astronauts to the surface of the moon from lunar orbit, and back again.

Originally lunar module LM-2 (opposite) was scheduled to fly the second test flight of the vehicle in Earth orbit. However, the first orbital test flight, flown by LM-1 in 1968, performed well enough that NASA chose to repurpose LM-2 for Earth tests. LM-1 had demonstrated crew compartment integrity, the descent and ascent engines, stage separation, and attitude thruster.

NASA managers decided to use LM-2 for drop-testing in Houston, instead of another orbital flight. Engineers dropped the spacecraft pictured here, from various heights and angles, to determine the impact that landing on a solid surface would have on landing gear as well as electrical wiring. Again, all the tests were successful.

When organizers of the U.S. Pavilion at the upcoming World's Fair in Osaka learned about LM-2, they requested the spacecraft. The fair offered the United States an opportunity to present a positive image of the nation's accomplishments at a time when the country was heavily criticized in Asia for its involvement in the Vietnam War. The lunar module exhibit, along with a moon rock and other space artifacts, drew a crowd of 18 million people to the U.S. Pavilion over the course of the World's Fair.

The media often compared the United States and Soviet Pavilions, as with *Kobe Shimbun,* a Japanese newspaper, which declared the United States "the winner in space competition" because its displayed real artifacts, including the ascent stage of LM-2. "In the end," the article noted, "it's the impact of real things. The Soviets also have a space exhibit. But they are models and cannot compare with the real Apollo." According to U.S. government

evaluations of the exhibit, the fact that LM-2 was designed for flight, even though it never orbited Earth or landed on the moon, made it a more politically potent artifact. LM-2, along with the other Apollo artifacts on display in Osaka, made the front page of all major Japanese newspapers, displacing news coverage of Vietnam.

After LM-2's exhibition in Japan, the Smithsonian Institution reconfigured it to more closely resemble the lunar module that had landed Neil Armstrong and Buzz Aldrin on the moon. In 1970, Smithsonian curator Fred Durant articulated the importance of such an exhibit: "A strong visual exhibit of this sort can be important in renewing pride in past space accomplishments and interest in the future." •

15 Command Module *Columbia,* Apollo 11

Date: 1969
Manufacturer: North American Aviation, Inc.
Origin: Downey, California
Materials: Aluminum alloy, stainless steel, titanium
Dimensions: 10 feet 7 inches by 21 feet 10 inches
Weight: 9,139 pounds

The Apollo 11 crew climbed into this command module (CM) a little before 7 a.m. on July 16, 1969. They had woken up at 4:15 a.m. sharp, eaten breakfast, and suited up at 5:35 a.m. An air-conditioned van transported them to the launchpad at 6:27 a.m. As they sat in the CM for more than two hours, waiting for launch, Mission Commander Neil Armstrong nervously tried to keep his leg

still. Although *Columbia* was spacious compared to the crew compartments of the earlier Mercury and Gemini spacecraft, Michael Collins, sitting next to Armstrong in the center of the three seats, noticed that the large pocket on the left leg of Armstrong's space suit, designed to hold the very first lunar rock samples, drooped perilously close to the T-shaped controller he would have to use to initiate an emergency abort sequence. It was just one example of how a simple design oversight, or a slight unplanned movement by one of the astronauts, could jeopardize the mission.

The Apollo spacecraft consisted of three parts: the command module (pictured opposite), the service module (SM), and the lunar module (LM). While the CM housed the astronauts in an area about as roomy as a family car, the cylindrical SM provided propulsion, power, life support, and the capacity (on later missions) to hold scientific instruments to study the moon from lunar orbit. The LM, which would carry

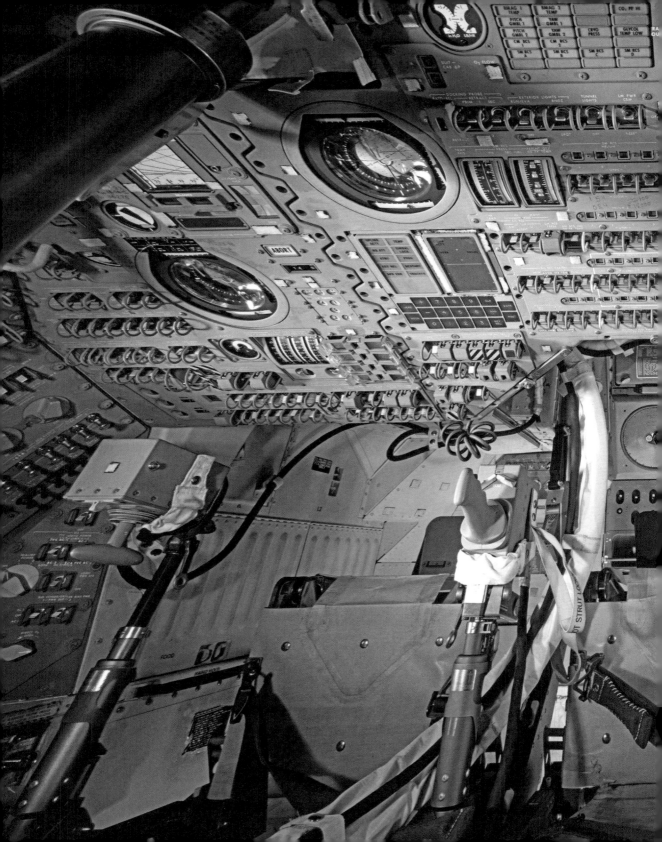

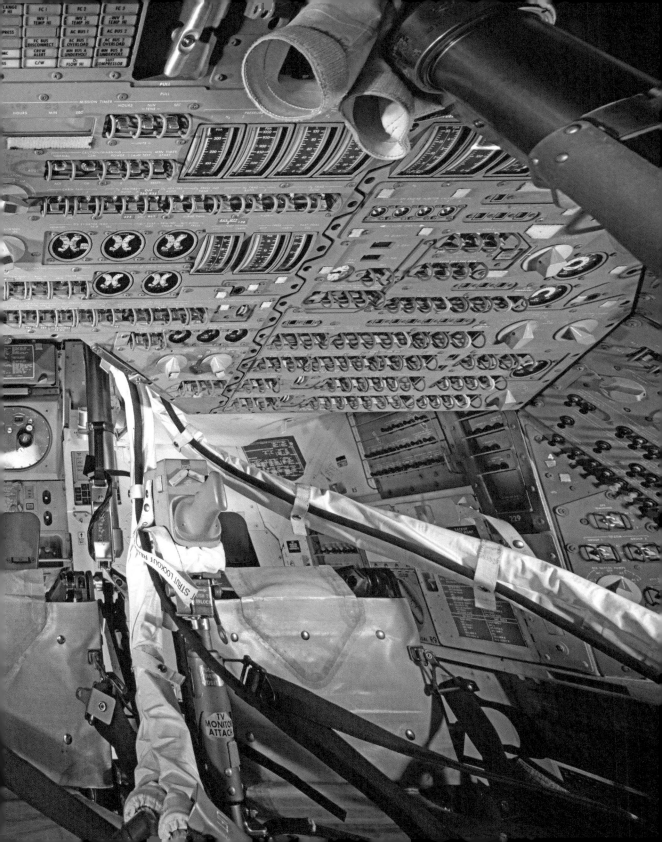

PAGE 96: The Apollo 11 command module served as living quarters for the crew for the duration of their mission in July 1969.

PAGES 98–99: *Columbia*'s main control panel is located above the astronauts' seats, as seen through the module's hatch.

"Yes, my happy little home, Command Module 107."

—Michael Collins, Apollo 11 astronaut

the astronauts to and from the lunar surface, docked to the CM's nose. In the end, only the command module was capable of safely reentering Earth's atmosphere.

Design of the CM began in 1961, when North American Aviation won the contract. Engineers applied the lessons learned from the Mercury and Gemini programs to refine this next-generation spacecraft. Although the CM's primary purpose was straightforward—to keep the astronauts alive and healthy—engineers faced many technical challenges, especially that of keeping the weight of the spacecraft down. The more weight, the more fuel that would be required to reach the moon.

Engineers reduced some of the CM's weight by creatively trimming the thickness of materials. For example, they made the heat shield that coated the walls of the module out of an aluminum honeycomb filled with ablative resin, rather than solid metal. Some reductions were operational. For instance, instead of creating a thicker heat shield to protect the side of the module facing the sun from solar radiation, a line of computer code was created to automatically rotate the spacecraft slowly during the transit from Earth to moon.

The microgravity environment allowed the astronauts to move freely above and below the seats, which many astronauts said alleviated the cramped conditions. However, it also meant that every task, from eating to going to the bathroom, required effort and training in the absence of gravity. Although a system allowed liquid waste to vent out to space, all other waste had to be bagged and sealed into storage lockers for the remainder of the voyage.

The Apollo 11 command and service modules as seen from the lunar module after undocking. The four parabolic dishes of the high-gain antenna on the upper left edge kept *Columbia* in near-constant contact with Mission Control—they lost connection when behind the moon.

While Armstrong and Buzz Aldrin flew the lunar module *Eagle* to the surface of the moon, Michael Collins remained aboard *Columbia* in lunar orbit. He stayed busy, checking navigation and photographing the lunar surface, as well as attempting, unsuccessfully, to precisely locate the *Eagle* through the command module's sextant. When he orbited around the far side of the moon, Collins was cut off from all communication with Earth as well as his crewmates. A NASA official commented during one of these passes, "Not since Adam has any human known such solitude as Mike Collins is experiencing . . ."

Armstrong and Aldrin rejoined their crewmate on *Columbia* 28 hours after they departed, after completing the first lunar landing and moonwalk. Without the *Eagle* perched on its bow, and with precious lunar samples safely stowed in lockers, the *Columbia* used the service module thruster to break lunar orbit and return to Earth, splashing down near Hawaii on July 24, 1969. •

Columbia's Graffiti

In the cramped confines of the command module, Apollo 11's astronauts frequently found it necessary to use whatever writing surface was available to take notes. Often, this meant they would turn to the walls of the craft itself. These collections of marks, notes, and numbers document both the work of space travel and details of everyday life in space.

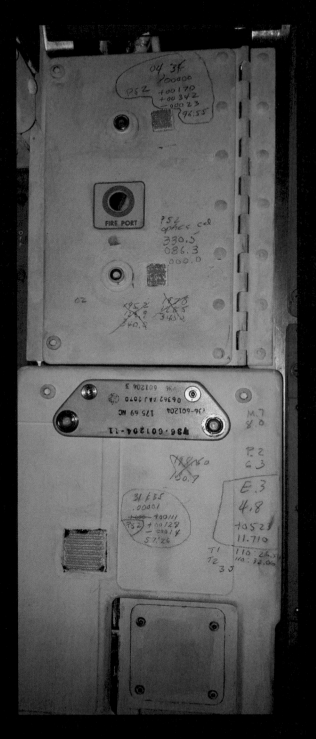

RIGHT: A series of notes representing coordinates on a lunar surface map, relayed by Mission Control to Michael Collins as he attempted to locate his crewmates' landing site from orbit

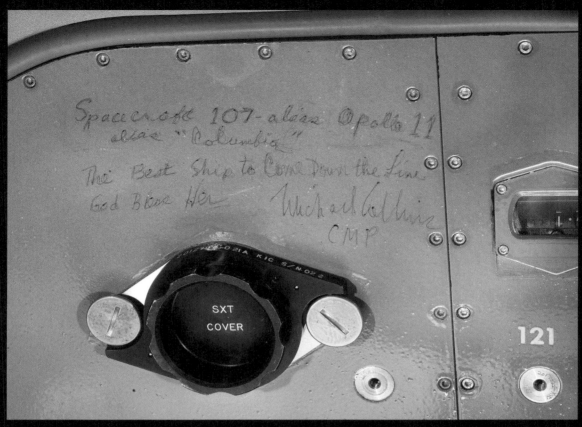

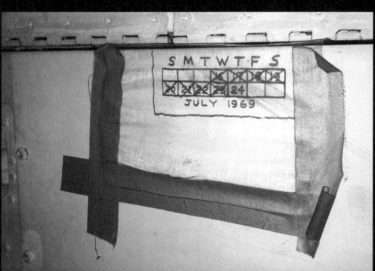

ABOVE: Michael Collins crawled back into *Columbia* while aboard the U.S.S. *Hornet* to inscribe a message on the navigational system reading "Spacecraft 107—alias Apollo 11—alias Columbia. The best ship to come down the line. God Bless Her. Michael Collins, CMP"

LEFT: The crew sketched a calendar counting down the days of their mission. At one point, they taped a piece of plastic over it, perhaps to prevent smudging as they floated by on their duties.

Liftoff!

Introduction

"We have a liftoff!"

Over a live television broadcast of the launch on July 16, 1969, came the countdown: ". . . six, five, four, three, two, one, zero. All engines running. Liftoff! We have a liftoff! Thirty-two minutes past the hour. Liftoff on Apollo 11!" The voice was that of John "Jack" King, NASA chief of public information. Known as the "voice of launch control," King described countdown events for every crewed mission from Gemini 4 in 1965 to Apollo 15 in 1971. For each mission, King's cry—"We have a liftoff!"—echoed out from Cape Canaveral, beyond the Florida shores, to every corner of the nation and the world.

During the 1960s, Cocoa Beach's population, already booming from the growth NASA brought to the cape, skyrocketed before every launch. Hundreds of thousands of people traveled to Florida to view each impressive liftoff. For the Apollo 11 launch alone, an estimated one million people descended on the surrounding area. But the impact of Project Apollo was not limited to tourism of the Space

A 1965 map of Cape Kennedy and environs shows the soon-to-be-built Apollo facilities on the far right and the close proximity of Cocoa Beach and other nearby communities.

Coast. The race to the moon converged with American society more broadly in the late 1960s, influencing everything from popular culture to politics to debates about the greater national purpose.

From the popularity of space memorabilia, toys, and launches to the protests of space expenditures, Project Apollo was an integral part of 1960s America—one important facet of the culture, politics, and an environment of change that permeated life in that era. ●

16 Mission Emblem, Apollo 11

Date: 1969
Manufacturer: Owens-Corning Fiberglass
Origin: Toledo, Ohio
Material: White Beta cloth with silk-screened emblem of Apollo 11
Dimensions: 3½ inches square

When Apollo 11 command module pilot Michael Collins designed his mission emblem (opposite), he was well aware of its potential symbolic and historical significance. Not only would it adorn the Apollo 11 flight suits, recovery suits, and jackets, it would also brand the mission, appearing on souvenirs, in newspapers, and on promotional material around the world. The distinctive emblem depicts an American bald eagle, a reference to the national bird as well as the name of the mission's lunar module, *Eagle.* Its talons clutch the long-standing symbol of peace: an olive branch.

NASA crews started designing their own emblems for mission patches in the mid-1960s. The first patch, created for the Gemini 5 flight in 1965, includes a drawing of a Conestoga wagon, meant to represent the pioneering nature of space exploration. Astronaut Gordon Cooper suggested adding the slogan "8 Days or Bust" as a play on the traditional frontier slogan "California or Bust," as well as to highlight the long duration of the mission. NASA rejected the slogan but approved the rest of the design.

When it was time to design the Apollo 11 emblem, the crew decided against adding their names, as prior missions had done. As Collins later explained, "We wanted to keep our three names off it because we wanted the design to be representative of everyone who had worked toward a lunar landing, and there were thousands who could take a proprietary interest in it." Instead, the design would be "symbolic rather than explicit."

The crew also debated how the mission number should be depicted on the

emblem. In his first rendition, Collins spelled out the word "eleven." Fellow crewmember Neil Armstrong argued against this design element, pointing out that if they used the numeral 11 instead, people from non-English-speaking countries could understand it more easily. When astronaut Jim Lovell suggested featuring the national bird—a bald eagle—at the center of the emblem, Collins flipped through a National Geographic book, *Water, Prey, and Game Birds of North America,* for inspiration. He then traced the outline of a bald eagle using a piece of tissue paper. Collins added lunar craters below the flying eagle, with Earth in the distant background. When Tom Wilson, an Apollo 11 simulator instructor, saw the draft sketch, he suggested adding an olive branch, to symbolize the peaceful nature of the mission. Collins agreed, drawing a branch held in the eagle's beak.

Robert Gilruth, director of the Manned Spacecraft Center, rejected this first draft, telling the crew to make the eagle less threatening. So Collins moved the olive branch from the eagle's beak to its talons.

Although this edit satisfied NASA officials, Collins felt the eagle appeared "uncomfortable," commenting that he "hoped he dropped the olive branch before landing."

The image of Earth as depicted on the emblem is technically incorrect. From the surface of the moon, Earth does look like a blue marble suspended in the blackness of outer space. But the shadow should appear at the bottom of Earth, not on the left side, as it is drawn. This mistake appeared in Collins's first submission and was never corrected.

All of the Apollo crews worked with A-B Emblem, an embroidery company based in Weaverville, North Carolina, on their patch design and production. The company first partnered with the space agency on the creation of a NASA "meatball" logo patch in 1961. The commander of each crew would fly to North Carolina to communicate the vision of the patch to the designers at A-B Emblem. These designers would then use scale rulers as well as an enlarging camera to blow up the graphic of the patch sixfold. In the next step, they marked the design with the location of each embroidery stitch, and the image was fed into a punching machine. The punching roll, created by the machine, was in turn fed into a Swiss embroidery loom. Each patch was then cut and given a pearl-stitched border.

Instead of using embroidered patches on the space suits designed for moonwalks, technicians silk-screened the crew's patches onto fire-resistant Beta cloth, which was then sewn onto the suit. The NASA emblem and the mission emblem bracket the astronaut's name badge on the chest of the suit, and an American flag adorned the left shoulder. Because NASA's Crew and Thermal Systems Division usually did not send off the mission patch until shortly before launch date, they were often hand-sewn on. This was done with a curved needle, to avoid puncturing through the insulation of the suit—another contribution by one of the thousands who had a hand in this mission. •

Apollo Mission Insignia

Designing insignia for units and projects is a military tradition that carried into the civilian space program in the mid-1960s. Administrator James Webb assigned crews the responsibility of creating their own patches. Each design is highly symbolic, representing the crew's goals, the specific mission, and, at times, the astronauts' humor.

Apollo 1: Al Stevens designed this patch—the Apollo spacecraft over Cape Canaveral—for a 1967 mission that never flew because of a fire during a systems test.

Apollo 7: According to Walter Cunningham, the crew's original design had a spacecraft called the Phoenix, "rising from a ball of fire."

Apollo 8: Jim Lovell's design, shaped like the command module itself, as well as the A of Apollo, uses a figure eight to represent both the mission number and its flight path.

Apollo 9: This insignia represents all three elements of the Apollo spacecraft, celebrating the first flight of the lunar module. The red-filled D signifies the launch's letter designation.

Apollo 10: This shield-shaped insignia, with the Roman numeral X planted on the moon, was the last Apollo patch to feature stylized space hardware.

Apollo 12: A nautical theme references the crew's shared background as Navy aviators. Three stars represent the members of the crew; a fourth honors astronaut C. C. Williams, the mission's original lunar module pilot, who died in a plane crash.

Apollo 13: This patch features three horses pulling the sun, homage to the chariot of Apollo, along with the Latin motto *"Ex Luna, Scientia—From the Moon, Knowledge."*

Apollo 14: In this ovoid insignia, the spacecraft is represented by a copy of the gold astronaut pin, worn by members of the astronaut corps who have been to space, such as commander of this mission Alan Shepard, the only one of the Mercury 7 to walk on the moon.

Apollo 15: Italian designer Emilio Pucci created the initial patch design for this crew, as he explained, with "three fast-moving elements in space in the form of a capsule closely flying in formation to indicate the common goal and purpose of [the] flight."

Apollo 16: The crew of Apollo 16 sought to symbolize teamwork, patriotism, and the moon in their patch; the 16 white stars represent the mission number.

Apollo 17: Artist Robert McCall modeled this patch on a sculpture of the Greek god Apollo in the Vatican Museums.

Apollo 1

Apollo 7

Apollo 8

Apollo 9

Apollo 10

Apollo 12

Apollo 13

Apollo 14

Apollo 15

Apollo 16

Apollo 17

17 Model Astronauts and Lunar Roving Vehicles

Date: ca 1970
Manufacturer: Airfix
Origin: London, England
Materials: Plastic
Dimensions: Astronaut: 1 inch tall

Airfix of London produced its Apollo moon landing model kit in 1969. It included 15 astronauts as well as parts for a lunar roving vehicle and a number of Apollo experiments, totaling 57 pieces in all. In some ways, it is an unusual boxed model kit, focused on a larger number of small playable pieces rather than containing disparate parts that could be assembled into one larger vehicle. A set like this harked back to play sets popular in the 1950s. Organized around a theme such as a battle, a time period, or another setting, those sets allowed players to arrange figures into playable dioramas. Such play sets often featured not only in a central building or backdrop but also two opposing groups of figurines: soldiers from different sides of a war, spacemen and aliens, or cowboys and Indians. In similar fashion, bags of little plastic army figures frozen in fighting poses became popular toys in the postwar period.

Molded in creamy white (as opposed to the traditional army green), the 15 astronauts in this set came in seven different poses. The astronaut pieces have small holes at their backs where the life support system backpacks can be affixed. Although not entirely accurate, these simplified models of Apollo astronauts let children—and diorama makers—re-create scenes like the first lunar landing in their own homes.

Space-themed toys like these model astronauts, and also Buzz Lightyear, *Star Wars* action figures, and more are now part of the Smithsonian Institution's collection because they reveal

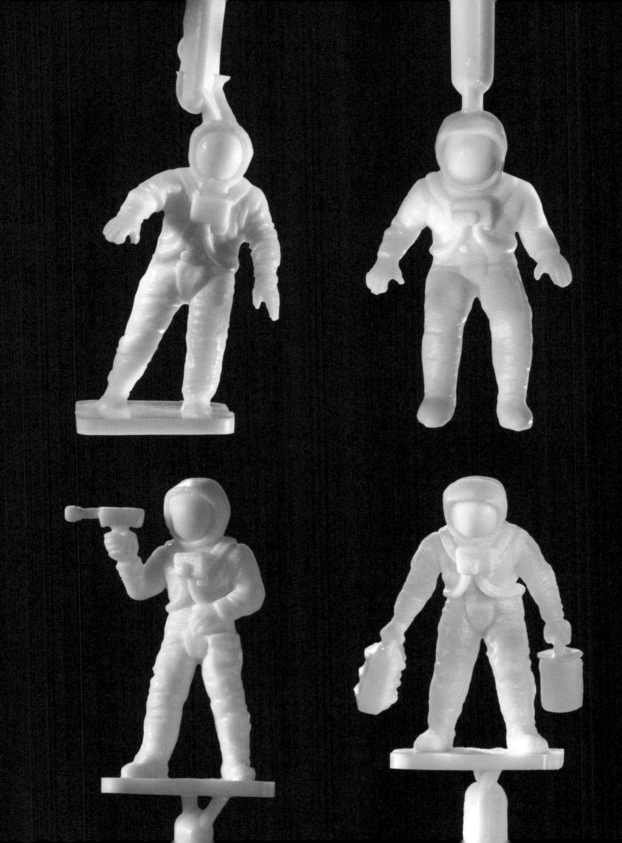

how people outside of NASA centers and contractors' labs have engaged with space exploration over time. They reflect the way the race for space affected popular imagination. The great enthusiasm for spaceflight led children, as well as adults, to create their own visions of exploration through play.

Moreover, these and other toys imagined alternate realities for space exploration in ways impractical for the Apollo missions. The actual lunar surface never had more than one mission on it. There were never more than two astronauts walking in space suits on the moon together. But this kit allowed enthusiasts to play as though the entire Apollo program—all 11 crewed missions, landing a dozen astronauts on the moon's surface—was happening all at once.

Founded in 1939, Airfix received its name in large part because the founder of the company, Nicholas Kove, wanted his company to appear at the beginning of business directories. After World War II, Airfix established its reputation by producing plastic combs using an injection molding machine. Branching out in 1952, the company started manufacturing scale plastic model kits for the mass market. The fact that a British company produced this set of astronaut models illustrates the wide geographic reach of Project Apollo enthusiasm.

As Airfax presumed, spaceflight toys appealed not only to Americans but also to all people around the world. By the late 1950s, space-age science fiction pushed out cowboys and Westerns, representing at least half of the $1.3 billion U.S. toy industry. Ray guns replaced six-shooters in the hands of children, the youth who grew up as the baby boomer generation, full of nostalgia for the Apollo mission to send a man to the moon. In the 1960s, with the rising popularity of hobby plastic modeling, Airfix added space-themed figures and vehicles to its growing line of military vehicles, engines, ships, cars, and military and civil aircraft figures. •

APOLLO 16

YOUNG · MATTINGLY · DUKE

RCA

18 RCA Sun Visor

Date: 1972
Manufacturer: RCA
Origin: United States
Materials: Cardboard, ink
Dimensions: 13$\frac{1}{8}$ by
11$\frac{1}{16}$ inches

This marketing opportunity was the brainchild of Nick Pensiero, a public relations officer for RCA (Radio Corporation of America). Known affectionately as "Uncle Nick" to many of his NASA and media friends, he realized that the liftoff of Apollo 11 was almost guaranteed to draw a record-breaking audience to Cape Canaveral, and garner global newspaper coverage, and he moved quickly.

Under his guidance, RCA produced 30,000 multicolored, cardboard sun visors much like the one pictured opposite. Alongside an image of the mission emblem, RCA was printed in bold, block letters. The slits down the middle of the hat created a dome when the ends were bent around a head and fastened. Uncle Nick initially hoped to distribute them at the press area and VIP site, but NASA balked at the idea. However, according to lore, a child found boxes of the visors in the back of Pensiero's car and started selling them to VIP visitors for a dollar apiece. After NASA officials stopped him, the visors were given away. By the time of the launch, the viewing stands were filled with spectators wearing colorful RCA visors. As hoped, a *LIFE* photographer captured the scene for the magazine's coverage of Apollo 11. Spurred by this success, RCA duplicated the visors for subsequent missions. RCA created this particular paper hat to keep the sun out of people's eyes during the launch of Apollo 16, which happened just after noon on April 16, 1972.

RCA had a long history with the Apollo program. In the early 1960s, NASA awarded the company a contract to develop a slow-scan, black-and-white

"It was clear to me that the American public was paying for Apollo and deserved as much access as it could get."

—Apollo Astronaut
Tom Stafford

television camera for the Apollo spacecraft as well as ground station devices that could convert the slow-scan feeds back into the normal American television format. The astronauts first tested out the RCA camera on Apollo 7, an Earth orbital mission launched in October 1968. In what became the first live television broadcast from space, the Apollo 7 crew showed the effects of weightlessness and held up playful written messages like "Keep Those Cards and Letters Coming In, Folks," and "Hello from the Lovely Apollo Room high atop everything."

Most NASA contracts left very little room for profit. But firms like RCA found ways to leverage their association with the space agency, selling both commercial and industry products by citing their use by astronauts. They also attracted new hires with the possibility of working with a cutting-edge team. After the success of the Apollo 7 broadcast, RCA's print advertisements emphasized the company's relationship to NASA. One that ran in national publications reminded consumers who already enjoyed RCA's brand of television: "You saw it 'live' from outer space, through the eyes of the Apollo TV system designed and developed by RCA."

RCA was not the only company leveraging its connections with the Apollo program. Grumman Aircraft Engineering Corporation, which produced the lunar landers, printed technical manuals for distribution among journalists. The handy volumes contained the craft's statistics inside—and the company name on the cover. In addition to ensuring that

media references to the lunar modules were accurate, the manuals put the company's name front and center on reporters' minds when they filed their reports.

John Bickers, who gave this hat to the Smithsonian Institution, wrote press reference books for space missions on behalf of McDonnell Aircraft Corporation (which became McDonnell Douglas in 1967), beginning with the Gemini Project. In addition to depositing his annotated versions of those data books in the museum's archives, Bickers donated his personal collection of spaceflight memorabilia, mementos of his work with NASA. For members of the public as well as for those fortunate enough to work in support of the Apollo missions, these were both sentimental and sought-after memorabilia. •

19 Crawler-Transporter Tread

Date: ca 1966
Manufacturer: Marion Power
Shovel Co.
Origin: Marion, Ohio
Materials: Steel
Dimensions: 7 feet 6 inches by
2 feet 1 inch by 1 foot 6 inches
Weight: 2,000 pounds

Before the Apollo program, it was standard practice to assemble and test staged rockets on their launchpads, often leaving the craft outside, exposed to the elements for weeks or months. To meet Apollo's ambitious launch schedule, NASA developed facilities to build Saturn V rockets off the pad, and move them to position on massive tracked crawlers. This steel "shoe" (opposite) is from the track of one of the vehicles that carried the Apollo spacecraft on the slowest portion of its journey to the moon.

To avoid the risks associated with building the gigantic Saturn V in the humid Florida climate, NASA constructed the enormous Vehicle Assembly Building, or VAB. This structure, over 500 feet high and with a footprint of eight acres, is still one of the largest buildings in the world. Its size allowed the entire Saturn V rocket to be assembled and assessed inside. In addition, engineers could service components from multiple spacecraft simultaneously in the VAB, allowing for much closer spaceflights, with fewer launchpads and crews. NASA staff determined it was safest to transport the spacecraft to the launchpad standing vertically. This meant that whatever transportation method they chose would have to carry a more than 300-foot-tall, six-million-pound skyscraper completely level for more than three miles. Rails were determined to be hugely expensive and complex to build, while a barge would be too difficult to control.

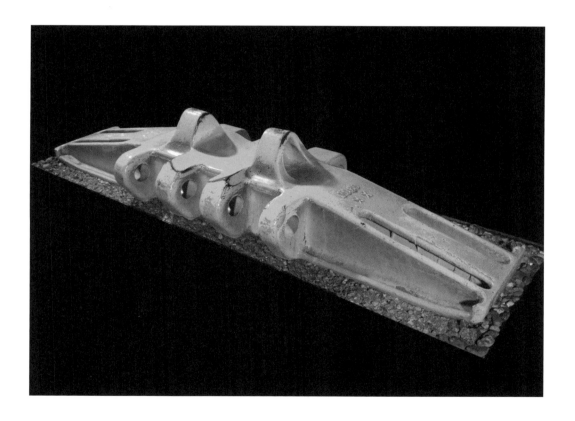

NASA engineers discovered a solution: the Bucyrus-Erie crawler-shovel, used to mine surface coal. This immensely strong vehicle had hydraulic controls to keep its work surface level, even over rough terrain. NASA awarded Marion Power Shovel Company, of Marion, Ohio, a contract for two custom crawlers. By early 1966, both vehicles were ready for testing. The crawlers weighed nearly 3,000 tons and were 130 feet in length. Two 2,700-horsepower diesel engines

The Apollo 14 spacecraft makes its way to launch-pad 39A on the crawler-transport on November 9, 1970, months before its launch in January 1971.

"I for one questioned whether a vehicle the size of Apollo Saturn could get out to the pad or not."

—NASA deputy administrator Robert Seamans

ran four double-tracked treads larger than a city bus, each with 57 shoes. Each shoe was seven and a half feet wide, weighing in at a ton by itself.

On top of the crawler sat the mobile launcher. This 90-foot platform held a tower that stretched the height of the Saturn V, with nine umbilical arms. During transportation, the launcher secured the rocket firmly, with the ability to provide it fuel and power through the umbilicals. Two high-speed elevators moved technicians to their workstations and brought the astronauts to their capsules.

In the days before a launch, a crawler picked up the mobile transporter at the VAB, and started along the crawlerway, a specially engineered track stretching the three and a half miles to launchpad 39A. A crew of roughly 30 drivers, engineers, and spotters helped the crawler move at speeds less than a mile an hour, running at 42 feet per gallon of fuel. After almost seven hours, the crawler's hydraulic lifts lowered the transporter onto the launchpad.

"When a man stands next to the crawler, the crawler looks big," observed Bruce Dunmeyer, supervisor of the Apollo 9 transporter team. "But when you see the crawler under the mobile launcher, the crawler looks incapable of lifting such a big load."

This track shoe is one of many refurbished and replaced on the crawler. Unlike the rest of the Apollo vehicles, the crawlers are still in use at the Kennedy Space Center. The same machines that transported the Saturn V transported the space shuttles for decades. •

20 SCLC Contribution Can

Date: ca 1960s
Manufacturer: Southern Christian
Leadership Conference
Origin: Atlanta, Georgia
Materials: Tin, ink on printing
paper
Dimensions: $2^7/_8$ by $2^7/_8$ by
6 inches

Organized by the Southern Christian Leadership Conference (SCLC), 500 protesters arrived at Kennedy Space Center (KSC) on July 15, 1969, a day ahead of the Apollo 11 launch. They had held an all-night vigil the previous evening. On the morning of the 15th, they made their way across a wide field near the western entrance of KSC, singing "We Shall Overcome" as they marched. The protesters walked alongside two wagons drawn by mules nicknamed Jim

Eastland and George Wallace, after the pro-segregationist southern politicians. In the lead was the Reverend Ralph Abernathy, Sr., who had assumed leadership of the SCLC after the assassination of the Reverend Dr. Martin Luther King, Jr. The protest sought to draw attention to poverty in America.

Most Americans remember the SCLC for the group's origins in desegregation efforts. Founded in 1957 after the Montgomery (Alabama) bus boycott initiated by Rosa Parks's arrest, and based in Atlanta, Georgia, the SCLC confronted segregation through boycotts, marches, and nonviolent protests. With the establishment of the Poor People's Campaign in 1967, however, its mission broadened to combat economic inequality irrespective of race. Many people do not remember that when Dr. King was killed in Memphis, he was supporting a multiracial sanitation workers' strike. This contribution can (opposite) was used to raise funds for the SCLC in the 1960s. Now in the

"If we could solve the problems of poverty in the United States by *not* pushing the button to launch men to the moon tomorrow, then we would not push that button."

—NASA administrator Thomas Paine

collection of the Smithsonian National Museum of African American History and Culture, the can depicts King and Abernathy, as well as the text "I Gave," which is printed on the reverse side.

At the gates of KSC, the group met NASA administrator Thomas Paine. As Paine recalls, "we were coatless, standing under a cloudy sky, with distant thunder rumbling." Joining Abernathy were 25 impoverished African-American families from the SCLC Poor People's Campaign, while dozens of newspaper reports and camera crews set up to record the encounter. Over a microphone, Abernathy explained, "On the eve of man's noblest venture, I am profoundly moved by the nation's achievements in space." But, at the time, one-fifth of Americans lacked adequate food, clothing, medical care, and shelter. "I want NASA scientists and engineers and technicians to find ways to use their skills to tackle the problems we face in society," Abernathy continued.

Paine responded, "If we could solve the problems of poverty in the United States by *not* pushing the button to launch men to the moon tomorrow, then we would not push that button." Even though Project Apollo required the most cutting-edge engineering advances of the day, he explained, they were "child's play compared to the tremendously difficult human problems with which you and your people are concerned." He invited the protesters to the VIP viewing

site for the launch and then added, "I hope you will hitch your mule wagons to our rockets," and use "the space program as a spur to the nation to tackle problems boldly in other areas."

President Nixon's adviser Peter Flanigan wrote Paine, thanking him for how he handled "a very delicate situation with consummate skill." He ended the letter, facetiously suggesting, "Now that you've handled the problem of getting to the moon, maybe you'd like to tackle those of urban affairs."

In the following years, NASA applied aerospace managerial practices and spin-off technology to the betterment of urban conditions. Conferences were held between engineers and city planners to discuss utilizing systems management techniques in urban settings. NASA research centers, in partnership with the Department of Housing and Urban Development, also investigated how to repurpose environmental systems for waste management and water purification. Although few programs progressed far past testing stages, the space program would prove effective in combating problems on Earth through other means, like the use of application satellites. •

In Flight

Section 5

"To see the earth as it truly is . . ."

In big bold block letters the simple statement, "3 MEN FLY AROUND THE MOON," ran across the front page of the *New York Times* on December 25, 1968. The crewmembers of Apollo 8—Frank Borman, James A. Lovell, Jr., and William A. Anders—had become the first humans to travel to the moon.

Along the journey they captured their experience on film to share with the global audience following the flight. In live broadcasts, and through still photographs of our home planet seemingly suspended in the inky blackness of outer space, the Apollo 8 crew communicated a sense of hope and unity. This message was all the more potent at the tail end of a year unhinged by the assassinations of Martin Luther King, Jr., and Robert F. Kennedy, with war raging in Vietnam and protests across the world.

Underneath the large headline, below the fold of the newspaper, famed American poet Archibald MacLeish reflected on the meaning of the flight. "To see the earth as it truly is," he wrote, "small and blue and beautiful in that eternal silence

This artist's concept illustration shows the separation of Apollo 8 from the S-IVB rocket on the way to lunar orbit. The four panels of the spacecraft lunar module adapter would, on later missions, reveal the lunar module.

where it floats, is to see ourselves as riders on the earth together, brothers on that bright loveliness in the eternal cold—brothers who know now they are truly brothers."

In addition to the scientific and technological achievements of spaceflight, Project Apollo had broad implications on what it means to be human. From the impact of spaceflight on understandings of humanity to the physiological and biomedical effects of weightlessness, lunar exploration expanded the bounds of human experience. •

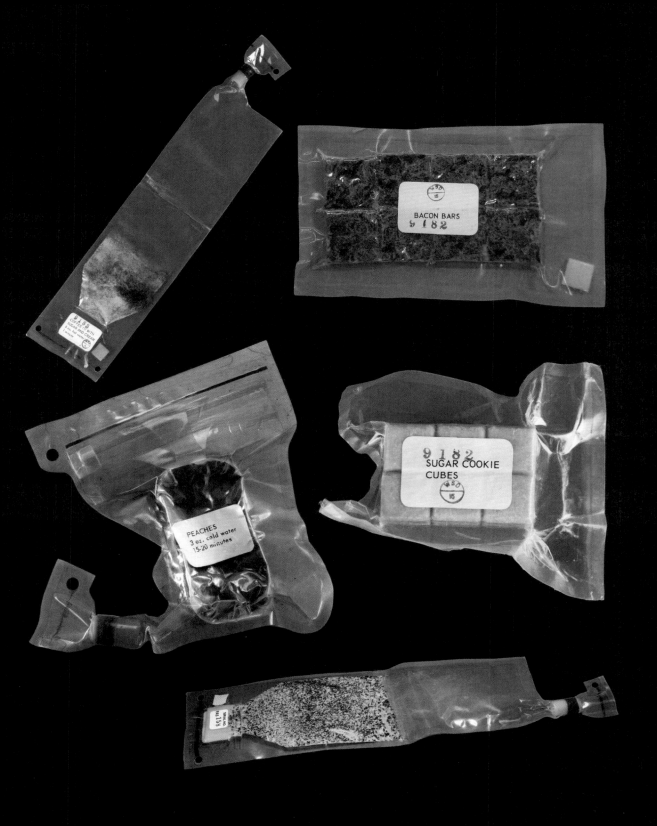

21 | First Meal on the Moon

Date: 1969
Manufacturer: Life Support Division of the Whirlpool Corporation
Origin: St. Joseph, Michigan
Materials: Plastic, Velcro, paper, preserved food
Dimensions: Dry packs: 4 by 3½ by ¾ inches; Wet packs: 5⅞ by 6½ x 1¼ inches; Beverages: 15 by 3½ by ½ inches

The first meal on the moon consisted of bacon bars, peaches, sugar cookie cubes, coffee, and a pineapple-grapefruit drink. After Neil Armstrong and Buzz Aldrin touched down on the lunar surface, and before they began the first moonwalk, they ate. Aldrin also used this brief break between mission procedures to take Communion. Technicians had packed four meals for the lunar landing portion of the mission. The second meal was hardier, with a menu of beef stew, cream of chicken soup, date fruitcake, grape punch, and an orange drink.

In the early years of American spaceflight, people were uncertain if humans could even eat in space. Tubes of applesauce, malted-milk tablets, and a beef and vegetable puree were included in John Glenn's Friendship 7 flight—not in the event that he got hungry, but to learn if a body could swallow and accept food in microgravity. Fortunately, there were no problems; Glenn joked that, provided floating crumbs could be kept under control, it may be practical to bring along a ham sandwich.

Several years later, when John Young and Gus Grissom secretly carried a corned beef sandwich on Gemini 3, the press and Congress asked NASA to more closely monitor what the astronauts put in their pockets. The official menus for Project Gemini were experiments in food preservation and reconstitution, palatable enough that crews would

"It's lousy coffee, but at least it's lukewarm and familiar, and reminds me vaguely of earth mornings."

— Michael Collins, Apollo 11 command module pilot

actually eat them but designed to provide enough nourishment and avoid such dangers as floating particles in the vehicle.

The Apollo food program brought huge improvements, and variety, over those of Project Mercury and Project Gemini. Perhaps the most significant development was the addition of hot water on the spacecraft. Using a water pistol, astronauts could rehydrate dry foods in sealed plastic packaging and then eat them with a spoon or through an integrated drinking tube. This new approach proved more reminiscent of eating a meal on Earth.

Flight menus were planned in close consultation with the astronauts. Each crewmember evaluated the offerings and made selections within NASA's nutritional guidelines. A typical day consisted of between 2,500 and 2,800 calories, with one gram of calcium, half a gram of phosphorus, and roughly 100 grams of protein. To ensure some variety on the missions, the menu was on a four-day repeating cycle. The meal packages themselves were labeled A, B, or C, for breakfast, lunch, and dinner, respectively. They also sported color-coded Velcro to identify which meal was for which astronaut: red for commanders, white for command module pilots, and blue for lunar module pilots.

For Apollo 11, food technicians added a few items to the menu: candy sticks and jellied fruit; cans of ham, chicken, and tuna salad; cheddar cheese spread; and frankfurters. They also introduced a "pantry system," letting

The cuff checklist worn by John Young during the Apollo 16 moonwalks. An engineer included a drawing of an astronaut commenting on an in-suit food bar, a long high-density bar for snacking on during moonwalks.

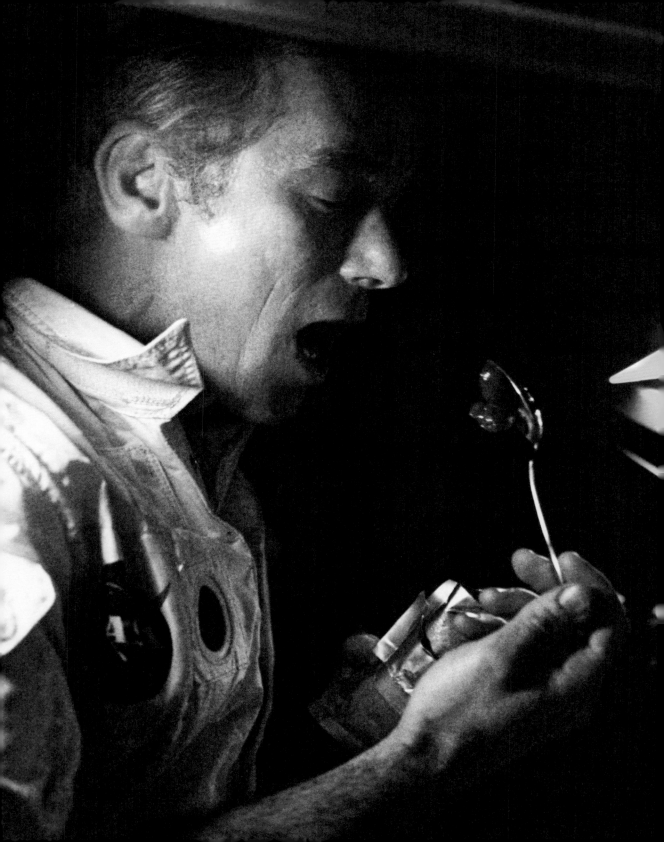

astronauts select their own food based on cravings and their appetites, including choosing from desserts of banana pudding, butterscotch pudding, or applesauce as well as a variety of candies. There were also drinks, breakfast foods, and entrées such as chicken stew and beef pot roast. Right before their flight, as they headed to the launchpad, each member of the crew placed sandwiches, bacon squares, and a rehydratable beverage into a pocket of their space suit, in case they became hungry during the first eight hours of the mission.

The food packages featured on page 136 are leftovers. Uneaten and returned to Earth after the missions, this selection joins nearly 500 other space food items in the Smithsonian Institution's collection that tells us about the astronauts' food preferences during their missions. "We have a lot of instant breakfasts," Smithsonian curator Jennifer Levasseur observed when assessing the collection. "I get the feeling these were the kinds of guys who just woke up and drank coffee." Less represented in the collection—probably because they were more likely to have been eaten—are the items astronauts liked most: hot dogs, spaghetti and meatballs, and shrimp cocktail.

In general, astronauts tended to eat less in space than they would at home. The Apollo 12 and 13 crews only ate 30 to 40 percent of their allocated food over the course of these missions—but not because they lost their appetites. The weightless environment causes fluids to circulate more evenly in the body, so an astronaut's sense of taste is dulled, making spicier and saltier foods more desirable. In addition, fecal containment units were awkward and unappealing to use, so minimizing the need wasn't so bad.

So, although the views aboard the Apollo spacecraft may have been spectacular and one of a kind, according to the astronauts, the coffee was not particularly good. •

Rita M. Rapp, Apollo Food System Technologist

As head of the Apollo Food System team, Rita M. Rapp made sure the astronauts would not only be nourished during their flight, but also satisfied with their food choices. As with many women who contributed to Project Apollo, Rapp overcame gender barriers to achieve a number of firsts throughout her career. She is among the scores of people who made the first lunar landing possible, but whose stories have not been widely known until recently.

Born in Piqua, Ohio, in 1928, Rapp earned a bachelor's degree in science from the University of Dayton in 1950 followed by a master's degree in anatomy from the Saint Louis University School of Medicine in 1953. Rapp was among the first women to receive such a degree. Saint Louis University School of Medicine started admitting women in 1949, when three female students enrolled. The first women to graduate from the school earned degrees in 1952, just one year before Rapp received her degree.

After graduation, she accepted a job as a physiologist in the Aeromedical Research

Laboratory at Wright–Patterson Air Force Base, east of Dayton, Ohio. There she assessed the effects of high g-forces on the human body, especially the blood and renal systems.

In the 1960s, she moved to the NASA Space Task Force to study how centrifugal forces impacted the Mercury astronauts. As she later recalled, the astronauts "would go to the School of Aerospace Medicine, for their annual physical and then they'd see me. They knew what was going to happen. They knew I was going to puncture them, bleed them about every four hours around the clock." Rapp also designed the first elastic exercisers for early spaceflight missions, developed biological experiments conducted on missions, and designed the Gemini program medical kit.

During Project Apollo, Rapp became the manager and later head of the Apollo Food System team. Their goal: to transform space food from "cubes and tubes" to items that more closely resembled meals on Earth. The team worked with Whirlpool Corporation to refine packaging, leading to the creation of spoon bowls and, eventually, thermostabilized food eaten out of cans. Rapp also took the astronauts' food preferences into account, explaining, "I like to feed them what they like, because I want them healthy and happy."

Along with division head and nutritionist Dr. Malcolm Smith, Rapp created menus to meet the astronauts' tastes and needs, often developing new recipes. When lunar module pilot Charlie Duke requested grits for his flight, he found, "it took her two or three iterations. By the time we got ready to fly, they were pretty good, so I ate all mine." Rapp was also responsible for the astronauts' meals at Cape Canaveral leading up to their missions, and was fondly remembered for baking dozens of sugar cookies. Rapp continued to innovate the NASA food system for the Skylab and space shuttle programs, and she authored or co-authored more than 20 technical papers on space medicine. In addition to the gratitude of the astronauts themselves, Rapp received the NASA Exceptional Service Medal for her work.

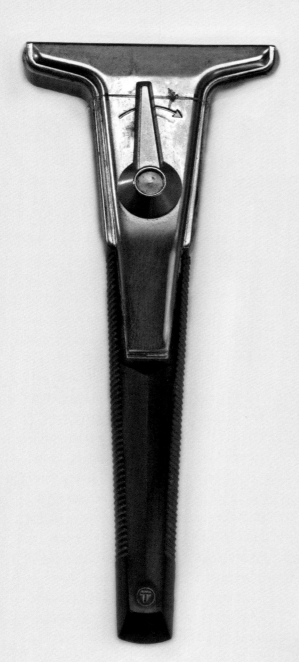

22 Razor and Shaving Cream, Apollo 11

Date: 1969
Manufacturer: Gillette razor company; Shulton Company
Origin: Boston, Massachusetts; Clifton, New Jersey
Materials: Plastic, metal blades, soft metal tube and cap
Dimensions: Razor: 4½ by 1⅞ by 1 inches; Shaving cream: 6⅛ by 2⅕ by 1¼ inches

"Things which were fun a couple days ago, like shaving in weightlessness, now seem to be a nuisance . . ." lamented Apollo 11 command module pilot Michael Collins. Nine days into the flight, inside a spacecraft that had become increasingly smelly and messy, lunar exploration had lost some of its luster. "There is no sink in which to wash the hair or even enough water to rinse the face," he continued. Instead, the astronauts wiped shaving cream off their faces with tissues and then endured hours of itching and scratching "to get rid of the last few whiskers." Collins was referring to shaving in space with this Gillette Techmatic safety razor and Old Spice brushless cream (opposite). Instead of requiring replacement cartridges, the razor's shaving head held a long thin blade, wound like a roll of film. When it dulled, an astronaut could twist the lever on top to advance to a fresh edge.

The first human spaceflight missions were brief, lasting for hours instead of days. On these short flights, concerns about personal hygiene—such as brushing teeth and shaving—were irrelevant. But as NASA started planning for longer durations, the agency faced questions about how to maintain the astronauts' health in space. Even though some Project Gemini missions lasted for days, and one stretched to two weeks, the compact spacecraft had very little room for anything more complex than washing with

PAGE 144: Michael Collins used this commercially available Gillette Techmatic safety razor and Old Spice brushless shaving cream during the Apollo 11 mission. The Techmatic cartridge held a long ribbon blade that unrolled to provide a fresh edge with a twist of the lever.

moist towelettes, and no equipment for heating water. After their two-week Gemini 7 mission, astronaut Frank Borman laughed that his unshaven crewmate Jim Lovell looked like a "bum recovering from a week-long binge."

Though shaving and other small rituals helped the astronauts maintain a sense of comfort and cleanliness en route to and from the moon, they also drew a sharp contrast with the counterculture movement of late 1960s America, which flaunted unshaven cheeks and long hair as visible symbols of political and cultural opposition. What NASA administrator Thomas Paine called "the triumph of the squares—the guys with computers and slide rules" clashed with some activists, who criticized Apollo for being part of the "establishment."

Grooming choices became so deeply politicized and emblematic of countercultural rebellion that the hit 1968 Broadway play about those themes was famously titled, simply, *Hair*. This small razor and its accompanying shaving cream remind us how grooming sometimes represents more than just a style preference. In the 1960s, for the military-trained men of the astronaut corps, facial hair was not just unstylish but also counter to regulations and expectations.

Although mission planners wanted to give their crews some relief, they feared loose hair and water particles would add to the already persistent problem of debris floating in microgravity. At the same time, in the aftermath of the Apollo 1 tragedy, NASA was attempting to remove everything flammable from the cockpit. Engineers tried without success to develop electric razors with vacuum attachments that would trap stray whiskers as the astronauts shaved. Wally Schirra remembered the suggestion that Apollo astronauts shave their entire bodies just before their missions. Noting the hair was going to grow back no matter what, he responded, "if the danger was such that hair was a hazard, then maybe I'd rather not fly the machine at all."

Ahead of his Apollo 8 mission in December 1968, Frank Borman requested that an electric razor be ready and waiting for him on the recovery helicopter. By Apollo 10 in May 1969, however, experience had shown that the capsules' air intake vents sucked up small particles and that foam and other viscous substances retained their shapes in microgravity. This allowed future crews to pack everyday safety razors and brushless shaving cream. Although the blades tended to clog with hair and lather without running water, shaving was otherwise possible—if not enjoyable. •

23 Urine Collection and Transfer Assembly, Apollo 11

Date: Late 1960s
Manufacturer: Whirlpool
Corporation
Origin: St. Joseph, Michigan
Materials: Neoprene-coated nylon,
natural rubber, Velcro, synthetic
fabric, steel, aluminum, elastic
Dimensions: 9½ by ¾ inches by
2 feet 7 inches

"Everyone has their first on the moon," reflected Apollo 11 astronaut Buzz Aldrin. Neil Armstrong had the first lunar step, but it was Aldrin who holds the title of the first human to urinate there. "That one hasn't been disputed by anybody," Aldrin mischievously commented in an interview. Unfortunately for Aldrin, his urine collection device (UCD) bag broke as he took a large leap from the bottom rung of the lunar module ladder onto the moon. As he walked, his left boot filled up with liquid. Each subsequent step Aldrin took on the lunar surface sloshed.

Buzz Aldrin's mishap on the moon was not the only time urine soaked an unlucky astronaut in their suit. As a NASA biomedical report understatedly observed: "Defecation and urination have been bothersome aspects of space travel from the beginning of manned space flight."

On May 5, 1961, when Alan Shepard was sitting in his *Freedom 7* spacecraft waiting for an inverter to be changed before launch, he faced a dilemma: He had to pee, but he was strapped into his seat. As Shepard later recounted, "we had been working with a device to collect urine during the flight that worked pretty well in zero gravity but it really didn't work very well when you're lying on your back with your feet up in the air like you were on the Redstone."

When Shepard asked fellow astro-

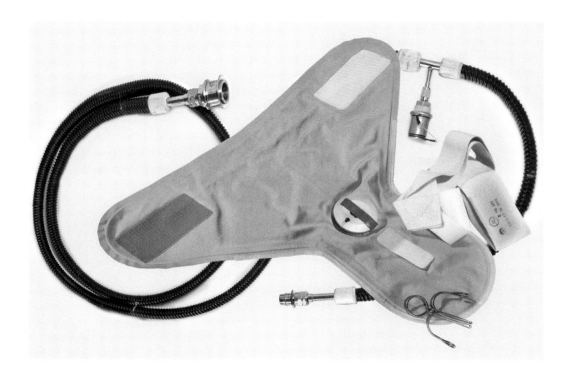

Astronauts wore this urine collection assembly inside their suits. The hoses moved the liquid into the yellow bladder and transferred it to the spacecraft's collection and dump valves.

naut Gordon "Gordo" Cooper, his CAPCOM (capsule communicator), if he could leave the capsule and relieve himself, "Gordo came back . . . I guess after there were some discussions going on outside and finally came back and said [in a German accent], 'No, . . .

[Wernher] von Braun says, "The astronaut shall stay in the nosecone."'" But what was originally scheduled to be five hours on the launchpad was stretching into eight. He suggested he relieve himself anyway. NASA engineers were worried he would short-circuit

149

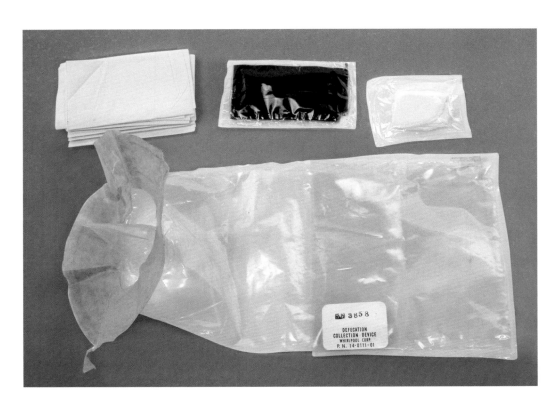

his biosensors. But at Shepard's request they briefly switched them off. This exchange ended with Shepard relieving himself, quickly soaking his cotton undergarment. Thank goodness, the 100 percent oxygen atmosphere in the capsule dried him off before liftoff.

Although Shepard's impromptu approach turned out fine for the brief 15-minute Mercury flight, it was clear the astronauts would need a better system for longer missions and extravehicular activity (EVA). On later Mercury flights, the astronauts used a rubber attachment linked to a flexible bag. A pump syringe created pressure, pulling urine into the pouch. But this UCD system leaked, and so engineers searched for a better design.

The model agreed upon for Project Apollo EVAs closely resembled the UCDs used for Projects Mercury and Gemini: They were equipped with rubber cuffs, a Y-shaped storage bag that would be tied around the hips, and included a "fecal containment system" diaper.

To handle human waste on board, astronauts used a cylinder attached to a hose, which was in turn attached to a urine dump port. A small opening caused a pressure differential, creating suction and giving the astronauts a feeling more closely resembling what they would experience relieving themselves on Earth. Not surprisingly for a scientific mission, a portion of the urine was freeze-dried and returned to Earth for thorough testing.

As the cuff of the UCD makes evident, all of the Apollo astronauts were male. This artifact is a powerful visual reminder of the exclusion of women from the Apollo astronaut corps. Although a private medical investigation evaluated American women as potential astronaut candidates in the early 1960s, and the Soviet Union sent Valentina Tereshkova into space in 1963, another two decades would pass before Sally Ride became the first female American astronaut. •

24 *EXER-GENIE*® In-Flight Exerciser, Apollo 11

Date: Flown on Apollo 11
Manufacturer: EXER-GENIE, Inc.
Origin: Fullerton, California
Materials: Straps: polyester webbing;
Handle: aluminum
Dimensions: 49⅝ by 1¾ inches

Apollo missions to the moon and back took more than a week. Even during this short period, astronauts experienced loss in muscle tone and mass as well as bone density. To counteract the physically degenerative effects of spaceflight, NASA engineers turned to the Exer-Genie (opposite).

The first series of spaceflight missions were too brief for astronauts to observe any serious physiological effects of weightlessness. John Glenn's orbital mission aboard Friendship 7 in 1962, for instance, lasted just under five hours. In preparation for the longer duration moon missions, NASA conducted medical tests as part of the Gemini Program. The longest flight, Gemini 7 in December 1965, gave NASA flight physicians an opportunity to measure calcium loss in astronauts Jim Lovell and Frank Borman's waste over the course of 14 days. This experiment, as well as the other medical evaluations conducted on Gemini missions, determined that astronauts could safely fly to the moon.

For Project Apollo, NASA purchased a controlled resistance device from Exer-Genie, Inc., in Fullerton, California. An off-the-shelf product first developed in 1961, the device was both lightweight and compact, fitting the engineers' criteria. Made up of an aluminum cylinder wrapped with nylon rope inside a metal tube, the exercise machine provided astronauts with adjustable conditioning levels to perform up to a hundred different exercises in space. They attached the two top

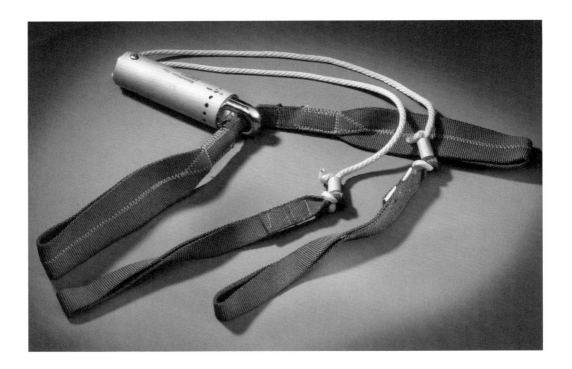

straps to the wall of the command module, set the resistance, and used the bottom straps, pulling and stretching at various angles and positions.

The crew of Apollo 7—Walter Schirra, Donn Eisele, and Walter Cunningham—were the first to test the Exer-Genie in space. The relatively spacious command module of Project Apollo allowed astronauts to stretch out more than they could in the cramped Mercury and Gemini capsules. The crew of Apollo 7 found that using it helped relieve some of the back and abdominal pain they were experiencing from sleeping curled up in the fetal position.

This particular Exer-Genie traveled aboard the Apollo 11 command module. After using it on the way to the moon, Apollo astronaut Neil Armstrong thought it "worked alright"—not a glowing review. Although NASA advised Armstrong and the rest of the astronaut corps to exercise for 15 to 30 minutes several times a day, Apollo 16 command module pilot Ken Mattingly thought the crew had far more important tasks than hooking up the device and pulling on the resistant straps. He argued that stowing space suits took more muscle power and was a better use of his time.

Even though these exercises prevented some bone and muscle loss, the crew faced other health dangers: Harmful cosmic rays bombarded the Apollo astronauts on their way to the moon, their hearts grew weaker from the ease of pumping blood in zero gravity, and some experienced slightly impaired vision. Although the Apollo astronauts mostly recovered from the effects of spaceflight shortly after their return to Earth, the biomedical threats of longer duration outer space travel continue to pose steep challenges for today's NASA engineers planning for future interplanetary travel. •

HORIZONTAL PRESS

Resistance: 15-20 lbs. Repetitions: 3
Time: 22 seconds Total Time: 1:06

Excellent exercise for increased strength and endurance in the upper arms and shoulder and building up the large pectoral muscles of the chest. Follow ISOMETRIC/TOTAL ISOKINETIC technique page 17, but move trail rope over handle and control with index finger of one hand.

Figure 80

Figure 79

Figure 81

42

SIT UP

Resistance: As indicated below Repetitions: 3 Time: 22 seconds
Total Time: 1:06

Increases strength and endurance in the abdominals and lower back. Follow ISOMETRIC/ISOTONIC technique, page 17, but revise to release trail rope after Static Contraction phase. NOTE: Set resistance so that 12 seconds is required to move through the range of motion shown.

DO NOT PERFORM THIS EXERCISE UNTIL YOU HAVE THE STRENGTHENED ABDOMINAL MUSCLES AND WAIST AREA THROUGH THE ADVANCED PROGRAM . . . i.e. FORWARD BEND AND SIDE BEND.

Figure 83

Figure 82

Figure 84

43

SIDE BEND (MUSCLE ISOLATION)

Resistance: 15 lbs. Repetitions: 3 (each side) Time: 22 seconds Total Time: 2:12

This is an alternate exercise to the SIDE BEND described in the Advanced Program. The muscles on one side are isolated and then exercised three times before proceeding to the other side. Use the ISOMETRIC/TOTAL ISOKINETIC technique, page 17. After the 10-second ISOMETRIC contraction, begin the TOTAL ISOKINETIC motion by pulling the torso erect with the muscles of the waist. Do not bend elbow. Keep it straight through the exercise. Repeat the procedure three times, then turn around on the floor piece and work the other side in the same manner.

Figure 86

Figure 87

Figure 85

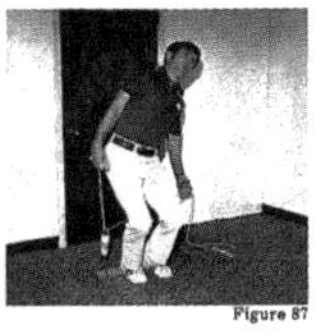

44

SUPPLEMENTAL EXERCISE

The Advanced Apollo Program outlined on the preceding pages includes all the necessary exercises which the average individual needs to use to get into shape and maintain an excellent fitness level. However, you can use the APOLLO EXERCISER and AEROKINETIC EXERCISE to isolate and exercise almost every muscle group in the body. Illustrated on the following pages are a group of supplemental exercises which will allow you to expand and vary your program. By maintaining the Advanced Program you can add these other exercises to work on specific areas of the body to help develop a more pleasing physical profile, and to further increase your strength, endurance and flexibility.

BICEPS CURL

Resistance: As indicated below* Repetitions: 3 Time: 22 seconds Total Time: 1:06

Increases strength and endurance in upper arm. Enlarges biceps. Use the ISOMETRIC/ISOTONIC, page 17, but revise to release trail rope at the end of Static Contraction phase.

*Resistance should be set so that 12 seconds is required to move through the range of motion shows.

Figure 77

Figure 76

Figure 78

41

HAMSTRING STRETCH

Resistance: 6-8 lbs. Repetitions: 3 (each leg) Time: 22 seconds Total Time: 2:12

Helps to stretch and lengthen the muscles in the back of the upper thigh to increase flexibility and lessen the danger of a muscle pull in this area. Follow ISOMETRIC/TOTAL ISOKINETIC technique, page 17, but revise to control trail rope with thumb and index finger of one hand or use opposite leg to control resistance. Alternate legs.

Figure 91

Figure 90

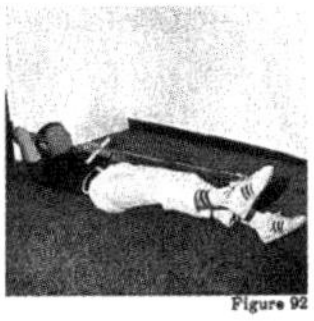

Figure 92

46

AEROKINETIC RUN* (Leg muscles, Heart, Lungs, Arteries)

Resistance: As indicated Repetitions: 3 Time: 90 seconds

This exercise adds another dimension to the AEROBIC principle of exercise. It applies resistance to the walking and running motions of the body, helping to increase the heart rate in a matter of a few seconds and maintaining it over the entire period of the exercise. When the running phase is implemented, one should experience a Target Heart Rate according to their age as indicated on page 75, recommended for effective aerobic exercise. In addition, this exercise develops strength and endurance in the leg muscles; another dangerous area of weakness among sedentary individuals.

1. Anchor exerciser in door waist high. Pull rope through until one handle is about one inch from the bottoms of the exerciser and secure harness as indicated on page 11 (Figures #10-10A & 11-11A).
2. Set resistance so that running action described in paragraph #3 takes 90 seconds to move rope through the unit.
3. Turn and run out at half speed, using high knee action, pumping arms (Figure #75).
4. If you reach the end of the rope in less than 90 seconds, adjust resistance upward. When you reach the end of the line, uncouple harness and set up on the other handle. Repeat a total of 3 repetitions.

Figure 75

*If it has been some time since you have done any continuous running, prepare by first following through the AEROKINETIC Walk, Shuffle, Run in the Beginning Program on page 27.

39

25 Hasselblad Camera, Apollo 17

Date: 1968
Manufacturer: Hasselblad
Origin: Gothenburg, Sweden
Materials: Aluminum, plastic, glass, Velcro
Dimensions: $3^{11}/_{16}$ by $5^{15}/_{16}$ by $19^{1}/_{8}$ inches

A mere five hours into the Apollo 17 mission, during a long string of observations narrated by geologist Harrison "Jack" Schmitt, the first photograph of an entirely unobstructed Earth was captured using this camera (opposite). This first image of the whole Earth, commonly called the "Blue Marble," became a symbol for an entire movement, encouraging us to look anew at a fragile orb set in the black emptiness of space.

Over 11 missions, Apollo astronauts captured some 18,000 still photographs using high-quality cameras built by the respected Swedish brand Hasselblad. This connection was all thanks to a fortuitous recommendation from astronaut Wally Schirra leading up to his Mercury flight in 1963. NASA, by tapping a non-U.S. manufacturer for such a literally visible contribution to the lunar program, associated some of the most profound and memorable images of the 20th century with both NASA and Hasselblad.

By the time of the Apollo 17 mission, the space program had increasingly come to depend on Hasselblad to provide flexible, durable, and reliable equipment that could be modified easily for the space environment. Hasselblad was more than happy to support NASA, working through its only licensed sales and service company in the United States, Paillard, Inc., of Linden, New Jersey. The special conditions of the spacecraft and lunar environment meant changes to the base model Hasselblad 500EL, including removal of unnecessary parts, replacement of lubricants to

Apollo 17's Hasselblad is pictured here with a 500mm lens, as it is now displayed. These long lenses were primarily used to capture panoramas of distant landscapes during moonwalks and from orbit. "Blue Marble" was taken with a smaller 80mm lens.

withstand cold temperatures, and the addition of tabs to make operation easier with space suit gloves.

For the Apollo missions, a battery-operated attachment was added to advance the film electronically as well as to record additional data. These HEDCs (Hasselblad Electronic Data Cameras) went with astronauts to the surface of the moon, and sometimes even

returned. Long believed to have all been left behind, recent research in NASA and other historical records shows four of the lunar Hasselblads (distinguished by their silver-painted aluminum bodies) made the trip back to Earth. The camera shown above, however, was a model meant for the command module only: simply a black aluminum body, lens, data pack, and magazine.

Officially designated NASA 22727, this image, taken while Apollo 17 was headed to the moon, became known as the "Blue Marble." The rare unobstructed image of Earth's surface was adopted as an illustration of world connectivity and raised environmental consciousness.

The visual story as told by the Apollo astronauts' photographs came to challenge our relationship with space exploration and our planet. "Earthrise" from Apollo 8 and "Blue Marble" both looked back upon Earth, but they came to symbolize entirely different perspectives. With Apollo 8, we approached and conquered the challenge of going to the moon, while the iconic image "Blue Marble" was taken up as the banner of the environmental movement. The photo inspired exploration of our home planet and initiatives to preserve it for generations to come. With little effort, NASA managed to provide concerned global citizens with the evidence they needed to encourage greater awareness of the human impact on Earth.

Poet Archibald MacLeish penned an essay, which was published on the front page of the *New York Times,* that captures the power of viewing Earth from space. "To see the earth as it truly is," MacLeish declared, "small and blue and beautiful in that eternal silence

"[W]e've only seen ourselves through the paintings of artists, words of poets, or through the minds of philosophers. Now we've been out there, we can see ourselves."

—Gene Cernan, Apollo 17 commander

where it floats, is to see ourselves as riders on the earth together, brothers on that bright loveliness in the eternal cold—brothers who know now they are truly brothers."

Cameras, the means by which these images were brought home, were critical for astronauts to capture and share their experiences. Today, museums use them as tools to tell the history of creating Apollo's visual legacy. •

Moonwalking

Introduction

"The heavens have become a part of man's world . . ."

At 11:49 p.m. on the evening of July 20, 1969, President Richard Nixon made what he considered "the most historic telephone call ever made from the White House." Speaking from his telephone in the Oval Office, Nixon congratulated astronauts Neil Armstrong and Buzz Aldrin as they stood on the lunar surface, reflecting "because of what you have done the heavens have become a part of man's world . . . for one priceless moment in the whole history of man, all the people on this earth are truly one."

As the president's message intimates, the Apollo 11 astronauts extended the scope of human experience in two ways: They landed on another planetary body, and more people came together to follow the flight's journey than any previous event in history. An estimated 650 million watched the television coverage of Armstrong's first step. It was the first ever live global broadcast, allowing people on every continent to view the mission in unison. Millions more listened to radio broadcasts or read about the mission in newspapers.

This map illustrates the landing sites of the six Apollo lunar landing missions, as well as the major regions of the moon's near side, called mares, or "seas" in Latin.

Humankind's first steps on the moon played out within a larger geopolitical context. Project Apollo was more than a scientific program or solely an American accomplishment. The lunar landings touched the lives of billions. ●

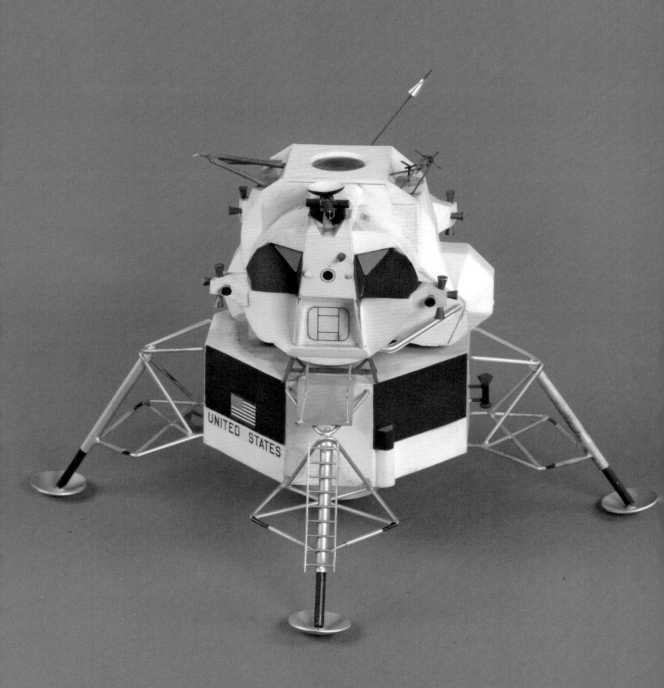

26 Walter Cronkite's Lunar Module Model

Date: 1969
Manufacturer: Thought to be
Precise Models
Origin: Cambridge, Illinois
Materials: Plastic, paint, aluminum,
adhesive
Dimensions: 7½ by 8 by 7½ inches

In July 1969, 94 percent of American households tuned their television sets to coverage of Apollo 11. Of these 53 million homes, the vast majority— including the sets at the White House— set their dials to watch news anchor Walter Cronkite, "the most trusted man in America," on CBS. As the Saturn V rocket lifted off from Cape Canaveral, the usually composed Cronkite sponta- neously exclaimed, "Go, baby, go!" Cronkite stayed on air for 27 of the next

32 hours of continuous CBS coverage, detailing each stage of the Apollo 11 mission. Because much of the flight was out of sight of film cameras, Cronkite used a small-scale model (opposite) to explain various stages of the mission.

The Eisenhower Administration's decision in 1958 to make NASA a civil- ian space agency with an open-press policy had significant ramifications for the media as well as for the public's awareness of spaceflight. From the very start, NASA welcomed reporters to launches, hosted press conferences, and gave out information packets to news agencies. When the time came to cover Apollo 11, CBS, as well as the two other television networks at the time—NBC and ABC—spent extensive resources over months of planning for their pro- gramming, recognizing that it would be one of the most newsworthy events of the century. At CBS, producers pre- pared 140 separate prerecorded clips, covering topics from biographies of the

PAGE 164: This model and ones like it were produced for Grumman, the manufacturer of the real lunar module.

> "I had to start from scratch because I am not mechanically trained in any way, certainly not scientifically . . . I took NASA's manuals and books, and I did my homework. I studied like fury."
>
> —Walter Cronkite, anchor, *CBS Evening News*

crew to an interview with former president Lyndon B. Johnson. A cadre of experts from various fields, as well as veteran reporters stationed around the world, weighed in during the broadcast. In total, more than a thousand people contributed to CBS's Apollo 11 coverage. At the center of the program, Cronkite anchored the broadcast, joined by retired Apollo 7 astronaut Walter

Schirra and science fiction author Arthur C. Clarke.

As an anchor for *CBS Evening News* since 1962, Cronkite had covered all the major news stories of the decade, from the assassination of President John F. Kennedy to the Vietnam War. His avuncular voice and calm delivery quickly became a national fixture. Before his television career, after hawking newspapers as a boy and studying journalism at the University of Texas, Cronkite became one of the first correspondents reporting from the World War II battlefront. In 1950, famed journalist Edward R. Murrow recruited him to CBS. A space enthusiast from the start, Cronkite shared his joy and knowledge of spaceflight with American audiences for years.

Despite his extensive preparation, when the *Eagle* lunar module touched down in the lunar soil, Cronkite could only cry, "Oh, boy!" before asking Schirra to say something because he could not. He quickly recovered, however, grasping the moment's extraordi-

Walter Cronkite uses a model of the lunar module
to explain the process of the moon landing to
his television audience on CBS.

nary significance: "Isn't this something! 240,000 miles out there on the moon and we're seeing this [on television]."

The model Cronkite used for his broadcast was commercially produced, most likely by the company Precise Models. Grumman, the lunar module contractor, distributed similar models to the media, dignitaries, and VIPs. The model was also available at the company store for $29.95. After the broadcast, CBS News associate producer Walter Lister "salvaged it to show [his] daughter and her classmates," eventually donating it to the Smithsonian Institution in 2009. Although the Smithsonian already had a similar item in its collection, when curators learned of its history, they enthusiastically acquired the Cronkite's model. •

27 Data Acquisition Camera, Apollo 11

Date: ca 1968
Manufacturer: Camera: J. A. Maurer, Inc.; 10-mm lens: Kern and Co.
Origin: Camera: Long Island City, New York; 10-mm lens: Aarau, Switzerland
Materials: Aluminum, steel, plastic, glass
Dimensions: 8³/₁₀ by 2³/₁₀ by 3⁶/₁₀ inches

At 102:31:04 mission elapsed time into the Apollo 11 flight, Buzz Aldrin pushed the flat black bottom of this 16-mm data acquisition camera (DAC) and started recording the first lunar landing. Aldrin had mounted the camera into a bracket inside the lunar module *Eagle* to film the scene outside his triangular window. This camera started

capturing *Eagle*'s descent roughly 15 minutes before the lunar module (LM) landed on the moon. When Neil Armstrong asked Aldrin, "Is the camera running?" and Aldrin replied, "Camera's running," Armstrong responded, "Okay, the override at five seconds. Descent armed."

NASA began using Maurer 16-mm sequence cameras during the Gemini program. This model, the 308, was modified slightly based on the performance during those missions. Its developer and manufacturer, J. A. Maurer, Inc., previously produced signaling devices during World War II, which prompted the development of 16-mm technology. Unlike television cameras, these sequence cameras were intended primarily to document mission tasks such as docking, undocking, and lunar activities. It successfully recorded these events, but it could not provide live news footage for audiences on Earth as there was no simultaneous sound recording by the camera nor broadcast capability.

Although DACs could either be handheld or mounted, as far as we know this particular one was only used mounted on brackets inside the lunar module. The L-shaped fitting on the right side of the DAC slid the camera onto one of two brackets in the LM.

A black button below the lens turned the camera on and off, and film magazines were attached on the left side. The DAC ran at lower frame rates than a typical movie camera, to maximize the collection of data while minimizing the amount of film used. It weighs

2.8 pounds with the film magazine attached. According to the Apollo 11 crew, the 16-mm images were closer to the true color of the moon's surface than the 70-mm still photography. As Armstrong later noted, "You can see these pictures, and kind of get an idea . . . a picture does a great job, but it's not nearly like being there."

A few hours after landing, Armstrong exited *Eagle* through the forward hatch and deployed an equipment module. As he descended the ladder, this DAC again captured the scene at 12 frames a second on Magazine J. But because of the angle of the landing, the shadow of *Eagle* fell across the view. While Armstrong stood on the ladder, Mission Control instructed Aldrin to adjust the camera settings: The recorded scene brightened just before Armstrong starts stepping off the ladder.

At 109:24 into the mission, on July 20, 1969, the DAC recorded a human's first step on another planetary body. Shortly thereafter, Aldrin exited through the hatch, descended the ladder, and joined his crewmate on the lunar soil. Once accustomed to the moon's low gravity, they set up a television camera at a distance from the lunar module to capture the scene for audiences back on Earth. This DAC also recorded the raising of the American flag on the moon.

According to the mission plan, this camera should have been left on the moon along with a great deal of other equipment to reduce the weight of *Eagle* for takeoff. Only the film canisters were to be packed for the trip home. After watching the footage the rest of the world celebrated, Buzz Aldrin jested, "Neil, we missed the whole thing." But Armstrong placed the DAC and other pieces of equipment in a Beta cloth bag, nicknamed the "McDivitt purse," and eventually brought the camera all the way home to Ohio. The bag and its contents were unknown to the world until Armstrong's widow, Carol, found it in a closet after Neil Armstrong died. •

28 Estonian Lunokhod Toy

Date: ca 1970
Manufacturer: AS Norma
Origin: Tallinn, Estonia, U.S.S.R.
Materials: Plastic, rubber, steel,
copper alloy
Dimensions: 12 by 5 by 8 inches

In mid-July 1969, Apollo 11 was not the only spacecraft on its way to the moon. On July 13, the Soviet Union launched Luna 15 on a Proton booster from the Baikonur Cosmodrome, a spaceport in western Kazakhstan. This was the 15th Soviet attempt in a series that would include 24 acknowledged lunar launches. Starting with an attempted mission that ended as a flyby as early as January 1959, and ending with a sample return in August 1976, the Soviet Luna program collected information about the moon for scientific studies as well as to help plan for crewed missions. The Estonian toy pictured oppo-site is a motorized model of the Luna program's Lunokhod robotic-rovers that explored the moon in 1970 and 1973.

Sergei Korolev, the "father" of Soviet rocketry, first proposed a robotic lunar program in the early 1950s, before any country had attempted launching objects into space. In 1959 alone, the Luna program accomplished three space firsts: the first probe to enter solar orbit (January 1959); the first probe to impact on another body (September 1959); and the first probe to take pictures of the far side of the moon (October 1959). But Soviet plans for human exploration faced setbacks, and by the late 1960s, the space program had set a new goal: a robotic sample return. The U.S.S.R. soft-landed on the moon, returned images and information on lunar soil (Luna 9, February 1966), orbited a satellite (Luna 10, March 1966), and captured surface photography (Luna 11, August 1966, and Luna 12, January 1967). After the United States successfully orbited astronauts around the

moon aboard Apollo 8 in December 1968, the Soviet Union planned Luna 15 for 1969. The robotic lander mission would collect soil samples and return them to Earth, preventing the United States from having a monopoly on lunar material.

On July 17, when Luna 15 entered the moon's orbit, it was scheduled to land two hours after Apollo 11. But its altimeter returned erratic readings of the target landing site. Soviet engineers analyzed the data and adjusted Luna 15's orbit, delaying its landing by 18 hours. The flight of Luna 17 in November 1970, with a Soviet Lunokhod rover on board, would prove more successful. Early plans for the Lunokhods were to support human exploration. They were to survey potential landing sites, and act as beacons for a crewed lander. On Earth, a team would control the vehicle with the aid of onboard cameras. By 1970, Lunokhods were no longer to support crewed landings: They were to head robotic exploration missions.

After Luna 17 landed in the Sea of Rains, Lunokhod 1 drove down the ramp and began a 10-month operation, remotely controlled by a Soviet ground crew, taking 20,000 photographs and driving more than six miles on the moon's surface. The solar-powered vehicle was about 7.5 feet long and weighed nearly a ton. A tub-like compartment with a convex lid sat atop eight independently controlled wire mesh wheels. During lunar day, the lid would open, charging the one-kilowatt solar cells. When the weeks-long lunar night began, the rover closed its lid and kept itself warm from the heat of rare and highly radioactive polonium 210. The vehicle also sprouted a cone-shaped antenna, a helical antenna, four television cameras, and devices to test soil. A second rover, Lunokhod 2, launched in January 1973, only operated half as long, but it covered nearly 25 miles until an accident caused the instruments to overheat.

This Lunokhod toy is a product of the Soviet republic of Estonia, with *kuukul-*

gur—its Estonian name (*kuu* for "moon" and *kulgur* for "runner")—prominently displayed on its box. The AS Norma factory in Tallinn, Estonia, was known by the late 19th century for making tin to can fish. After 20 years of independence, Estonia was annexed by the Soviet Union during World War II, and the company was nationalized. By 1966, toys had become the majority share of Norma's business, as leisure activity and an increase of consumerism became more common in Soviet life. The period saw a rising level of consumer goods and greater economic optimism from the previous turbulent decades. Likewise, space toys based on actual hardware fed into the grassroots interest in cosmic stories that existed in Soviet culture well before the space race. •

175

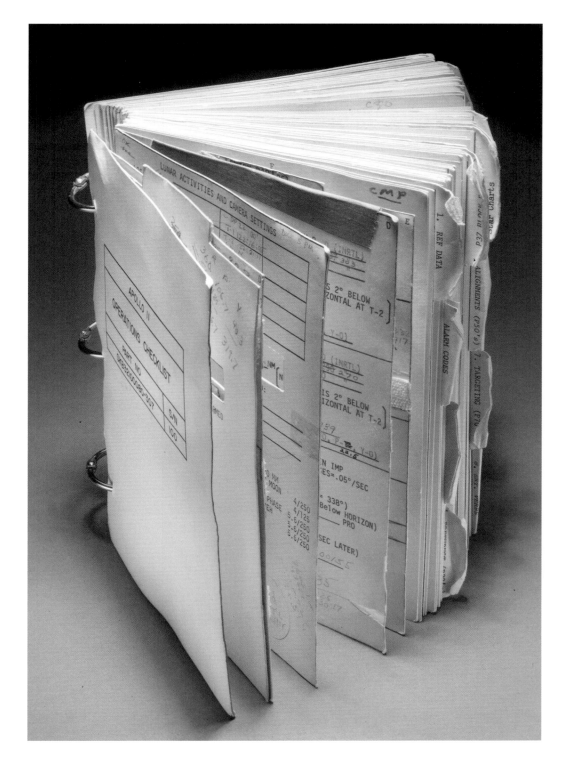

29 Command Module Operations Checklist

Date: 1969
Manufacturer: NASA, Manned Spacecraft Center
Origin: Houston, Texas
Materials: Paper, ink, steel, chrome plating, Velcro, adhesive
Dimensions: $7^1/_{10}$ by $1^6/_{10}$ by $8^3/_{10}$ inches

Project Apollo often brings to mind cutting-edge technology. But much of the equipment and procedures used to safely send astronauts to the moon and back were old-fashioned—even archaic. Apollo 11 command module pilot Michael Collins's operations checklist is one such example. As historian Matthew Hersch observed, checklists were one of the "constellation of 'small' technologies that made spaceflight possible." A centuries-old technology, checklists formed an essential link between the spacecraft's electromechanical systems and the astronauts. Along with the navigation aids and data cards, checklists were so critical to operating the spacecraft that Collins referred to them as the "fourth crew member whose views had to be considered."

In the 1930s, as airplanes became more sophisticated, pilots increasingly relied on checklists for preflight and takeoff procedures. Test pilots flying in the mid-20th century authored many of these checklists, enabling less experienced pilots to confidently and safely operate the new airplanes. During Project Mercury, astronauts used printed procedures on cards and small checklists tacked above the spacecraft's periscope. By Project Gemini, procedures including rendezvous and docking were more complex, prompting the development of the first onboard computers and more elaborate checklists.

Project Apollo moon missions required that the astronauts manage two

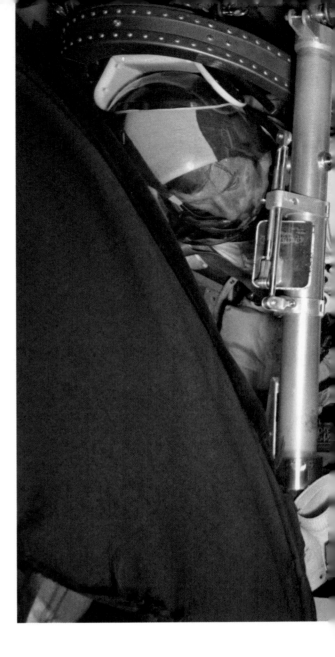

spacecraft with four modules, adding even more complexity to their jobs. Engineers designed a system where the digital electronic computers worked in concert with the crew, simultaneously monitoring reliability and validating human decisions and operations during the missions. Astronauts might be best classified as a new kind of engineer–manager, as opposed to daring pilots flying by skill and instinct.

NASA refined checklists over years of trial and error in flight simulators. Largely prepared by the astronauts themselves, they provided necessary step-by-step and switch-by-switch procedures. Detailed instructions also included reminders like when to wash their hands or that they should remove watches from pressure suits before they were stowed. Mission Control radioed supplementary instructions for the crew during the flight. One Apollo computer designer suggested that checklists were like a software program designed for humans instead of machines.

Collins used the checklist on page 176 aboard Apollo 11 in July 1969. Its 216 pages are divided into 15 "chapters" or sections: reference data, guidance and navigation computer, navigation, pre-thrust, thrusting, alignments, targeting, extending verbs (for display and key-

board), stabilization and control system general actions, systems management, lunar module interface, contingency extravehicular activity (a page missing from the artifact), lunar-orbit insertion aborts, flight emergency, and crew logs.

A Velcro lining allowed it to be stuck in a number of locations around the spacecraft. The paper is fireproof, a provision put into place after the Apollo 1 tragedy. In addition to this checklist, NASA equipped the Apollo 11 crew with

Ye Ole Lunar Scratch Pad

USE A & B for PTC

.03 O/hr x 5 hrs
.006 ft/sec

3 ACCEL CMD
TURN ON ECS
RATE CMD

5k ANT SEC + CMC

URINE
PARTICLES
LIKE ANGELS

TV
R 261°
P 010
Y 000
& HVA + P, VYB°

20° Y CAL CL (15)°
+ CSM oriee
P 2-20

V 49
70 MM
300 EXP FLM
1000 II CSM

24480
09152
00012

TV
R 261°

24 521
00 922
35998

NIGHT TIME: PUT FLOOD LTS ON (FAA)
DROP 250 MM LENS INTO BAG
SPOON UPSIDE DN.
INTO COMPARTMENTS UNDER COUCH w/o COUCH BEING THERE

TEC: J, 5   7.8
Recc9 P + 30
HGA   Y 270

LIMEADE
ICE TEA

Fresh Underwear
Helmet Protector

ROCK BOXES
FOOD
WATER + SPON
WATER GUN - WINDSKINS

FINGERNAIL
CLIPPERS

EV Visible Bmk
5+ MISC A-8
LCG Into Suit bag

LOOKS SIMPLE - NOT SO - LAUNCH VEHICLES
98,000 word VOCAB
SWITCHES > 300 + etc
SPS must Light or Scrounged
CHUTES MUST OPEN
HAD CONFIDENCE
HAVE

ENTRY
1500 NM
130/9N 169.10'W

ALL THIS IS POSSIBLE
ONLY THRU B, S, & T OF MANY
AMERICAN WORKMEN AT THE VARIOUS
PAINSTAKING TEST PRETEST AT FACTORIES
MSC MANAGEMENT, MSN PLAN FOR SWELL
PERISCOPE OF A SUB   TRIG

letter-size data cards, three-ring binders, and a Launch Operations Checklist.

Collins's checklist bears handwritten notes and annotations about navigation and systems monitoring. On the inside and rear covers, Collins identified the contents of each of the film magazines, noting the location of particularly interesting photographs. And at the end of the checklist are a number of foldout pages personalized for the astronauts, with Snoopy cartoons signed by engineers. Snoopy, the beagle from Charles Schulz's "Peanuts" cartoon strip, had become the unofficial mascot of the Apollo program. In one drawing, he is perched on a doghouse meant to represent the Apollo spacecraft. Stick-figure astronauts are drawn smuggling personal items on board.

In another playful addition, "Ye Ole Lunar Scratch Pad" is written in gothic black script at the top of one page, calling attention to how the checklist represents the convergence of modern and antiquated technology. On this same page, Collins mused "URINE PARTICLES

"And we have checklists for everything we did, even how to go to the bathroom there's a checklist!"
— Dick Gordon, Apollo 12 command module pilot

LIKE ANGELS," and jotted down notes for a broadcast scheduled during the crew's return to Earth. But the main role of the checklists was to help the astronauts manage the sophisticated technology. As Collins noted on Apollo 11's return trip on July 23, the spacecraft was essentially a computer with a "38,000-word vocabulary." In his hand was a switch "with over 300 counterparts in the command module alone," and myriad "circuit breakers, levers, rods and other associated controls." The checklist joined human and machine together into an effective integrated system. •

30 Apollo Flagpole and American Flag

Date: Early 1970s
Manufacturer: NASA, Manned Spacecraft Center
Origin: Houston, Texas
Materials: Pole: anodized aluminum, steel, paint, adhesive, plastic, lead, copper; Flag: fabric
Dimensions: 29 by 47 inches

Debate about planting a flag into the lunar surface roiled Washington during the weeks leading up to the first lunar landing. Although American flags had appeared on spacecraft, rockets, and space suits for years, raising a flag on the moon presented a new political dilemma. It was not until Congress threatened NASA's funding that the agency added the planting of a U.S. flag to the Apollo 11 astronauts' moonwalk schedule. The decision was reached just in time, with-

out a day to spare. Technicians installed a stainless steel case with an American flag inside on the ladder of the lunar module at 4 a.m. on launch day, July 16, 1969. Four days later, Neil Armstrong and Buzz Aldrin raised it on the moon.

A number of months earlier, NASA administrator Thomas Paine assembled a Symbolic Activities Committee. With representatives from a handful of agencies, this group planned the commemorative and public gestures that the astronauts would perform during their mission. When the question arose whether or not to place an American flag on the moon, the committee considered two options. The astronauts could leave a flag, or an adaption of the solar wind experiment in the form of an American flag, on the moon. Or the astronauts could leave a set of miniature flags from all nations, along with a commemorative marker.

U. Alexis Johnson, then undersecretary of state, worried that if the astronauts planted an American flag on the

moon, it would be seen as a gesture of territorial possession. He warned that even though the 1967 United Nations Outer Space Treaty established that no nation could claim sovereignty of the moon, an international controversy might still arise. The "raising of an American flag would seem most undesirable, since such an action has historically symbolized conquest and territorial acquisition." Officials at the United States Information Agency (USIA), which was responsible for the public and cultural diplomacy, agreed. They suggested that to "neutralize the effect of the American flag" planted on the moon, the astronauts should raise a United Nations flag beside it.

As the U.S. House of Representatives discussed NASA's appropriations bill for the fiscal year 1970, debate about the flag intensified. Numerous members of Congress weighed in, arguing that because U.S. taxpayers funded Project

Apollo, the astronauts should raise only a U.S. flag, and not a United Nations flag, on the moon.

Meanwhile, three months before the first lunar landing, Jack Kinzler, chief of the Technical Services Division at the Manned Spacecraft Center (now Johnson Space Center), started designing a flag assembly that could be raised on the moon in a bulky space suit. Known as "Mr. Fix-it," Kinzler had the attitude

that "whenever we get in trouble, that's when I get really interested."

Given the moon's almost nonexistent atmosphere, Kinzler added a horizontal crossbar at the top of the flag, which would create the illusion of a flag flying in the wind. He also designed a telescoping two-part pole to keep the assembly compact. Taking a standard three-by-five-foot nylon flag from a government supply catalog, Kinzler sewed a hem along its top for the crossbar. Kinzler knew that, because the astronauts' suits were pressurized to around 3.7 pounds per square inch, the amount of force the astronauts could exert on the flagpole would be limited. So he added a hardened steel point to the bottom of the pole to make it easier to plant.

Because the flag would be mounted to a leg of the lunar module, it had to be protected from the spacecraft engines, which generated temperatures up to 2000°F. NASA's Structures and Mechanics Division developed a stainless steel outer case, lined with Thermoflex insulation. They then wrapped the assembled flag with several layers of thermal blankets before placing it in the case. The 12-step process of readying the flag for flight took five people, and the aid of wooden blocks and plastic ties. The flag cost $5, the tubing another $75, and the protective shroud several hundred dollars more.

On June 10, 1969, NASA notified members of Congress that a U.S. flag, and not a United Nations flag, would be placed on the moon. That same day, the House of Representatives approved the appropriations bill, after amending it to include the following provision: "the flag of the United States, and no other flag, shall be implanted or otherwise placed on the surface of the moon, or on the surface of any planet, by members of the crew of any spacecraft . . . as part of any mission . . . the funds for which are provided entirely by the Government of the United States."

The flag pictured here reflects a design change for the missions following Apollo 12. After Charles "Pete" Conrad and Alan Bean had difficulty getting the horizontal crossbar's hinge to latch properly, NASA created a double-action latch, allowing the flag to stay raised even if the crossbar was not lifted above a 90-degree angle. All six flags that Apollo astronauts raised on the moon remain, although their stars and stripes have been bleached white by solar radiation. •

31 Eugene Cernan's Space Suit, Apollo 17

Date: 1972
Manufacturer: International Latex
Corporation
Origin: Dover, Delaware
Materials: Beta cloth, Chromel-R,
nylon, polyester, aluminum, Velcro,
rubber/neoprene, Mylar
Dimensions: 71 by 29 by 15 inches

Eugene Cernan was the last person to set foot on the moon. His space suit became the last human-worn object to set foot on the moon. Designed specifically for Cernan, the suit bears the red stripes on the upper arms and legs that identity him as the commander of the mission. The Apollo 17 mission emblem, along with Cernan's name and the NASA "meatball" logo, are sewn across the chest. An American flag sits at the left shoulder. Cernan's suit, like the ones that all moonwalkers wore, protected him from the harsh elements of outer space.

In the 1930s, risk-taking aviators attempting to set record-breaking flights learned that they needed suits that compensated for the thinner atmospheres in higher altitude. Pilots risked dizziness and even losing consciousness when flying at the high altitudes that would accommodate faster speeds. Later, with the widespread use of jet aircraft, they learned that supersonic speeds could drain blood from their brain to pool in their legs, potentially causing blackouts. These pilots soon adapted, lacing themselves into lower body garments to stave off pressures placed on bodies during high-flying maneuvers. By the 1950s, all high-performance pilots wore flight suits that supplied emergency oxygen and lower body pressure.

When President Kennedy proposed Project Apollo in 1961, space suit technology was in its infancy. Project Mercury astronauts wore suits that B. F.

Goodrich designed for the Navy, modified for use in space. In addition to matching the life support system to the spacecraft, an aluminum coating was applied for thermal protection and reflectivity and pumped air through the suits for temperature control. But these flight suits were built only for emergency use in case of spacecraft system failure. Functional for short flight, they limited mobility and primarily served as backup in the event that the spacecraft's life support systems failed. Gemini suits, based on Air Force pilots' suits, were more flexible but still not viable for lunar EVAs. Until this time, no one had built a suit that would preserve life in the

vacuum of space and allow an astronaut to walk autonomously on another world.

NASA held a suit competition in 1962, and then again in 1965, hoping that a contractor could find a way to keep astronauts protected from extreme environments and temperatures, but still make a suit flexible enough for mobility on the moon. The Special Products Division of the International Latex Corporation (ILC) met the challenge, building the Apollo suits from as many as two dozen layers of 11 types of materials. Cernan's custom-made extravehicular (or EV) suit configuration was the A7-LB (Apollo, 7th series, ILC, B-modification) space suit. It has a diagonal zipper that

PAGE 187: Eugene Cernan's space suit, still dirtied with lunar dust from his Apollo 17 moonwalks

OPPOSITE: Cernan operates the lunar rover in the Taurus-Littrow valley after unstowing it from the lander.

wraps around his torso. This style suit, with its additional flexibility at the waist, was created for Apollo 15, 16, and 17, missions where astronauts would be driving the lunar rover. Modified and slightly heavier life support systems used on these same missions extended the astronauts' EVA time from six to seven hours. Cernan's EV suit totaled a substantial 212 pounds.

To dress in a space suit, an astronaut began with a cotton and synthetic "comfort layer" (underwear), followed by an elastic bodysuit strung with water tubes—the liquid cooling garment that kept the astronaut's body temperature stable. The innermost layer of the pressure suit itself was made of a soft nylon, followed by the pressure layer of the suit: synthetic, woven cloth that had been dipped into a mixture of synthetic and natural rubber, its seams sealed with rubberized bias tape. To keep the suit's shape under pressure, a series of metal and cloth shapers and pulleys reinforced its general form while allowing astro-

nauts to bend their arms, legs, and waist. On top came more layers, made of nylon and Dacron, Beta Marquisette, and Mylar film, which prevented penetrating particles from puncturing the suit.

The most visible part of the suit, the outer layers, are made from Beta cloth, a wearable fiberglass. Red and blue anodized aluminum connectors allow for air outtake and intake, and for communications connections. The portable life support system was attached to the suit via the hoses. It controlled suit pressure, removed carbon dioxide, filtered moisture, equipped astronauts with enough oxygen for a moonwalk, recorded their life signs, and managed communications. Communications earphones and mouthpieces were worn on a flight cap, affectionately called a "Snoopy cap," after the comic strip character. The pressure helmet, a polycarbonate dome, allowed for full head movement and visibility. Finally came the distinctive gold visor, fit over the pressure helmet. •

Lunar Science

Section 7

"A geologist up here would just go crazy . . ."

As the Apollo 11 spacecraft swung around the far side of the moon, the sight of its densely cratered surface awed the crew. "Golly damn! A geologist up here would just go crazy," declared Michael Collins to his crewmates. The surface looked "plaster of paris gray," to Collins, pockmarked and full of mountains.

The Apollo 11 crew, as well as the subsequent crews that visited the moon, had trained with geologists for months before their flight. Viewing the lunar surface from that perspective, Collins, Neil Armstrong, and Buzz Aldrin discussed the dark flat plains and heavily cratered highlands ahead of the first lunar landing.

Science, and geology in particular, was a fundamental component of Project Apollo. In six lunar landings, astronauts took more than 1,500 pounds of experiments to the moon, and brought back almost 850 pounds of moon rocks, core samples, dust, and pebbles for study. Aided by lunar rovers, the crews of Apollo 15, 16, and 17—the most scientifically complex of the program—stayed on the moon longer, had greater

NASA-66-10989

EXPLORATION OF LUNAR SURFACE

mobility, and collected even more samples for scientific studies than previous missions.

In a program where every ounce of weight and each minute of astronaut time were at a premium, advocates labored to put meaningful science on the missions. Their efforts paid off through discoveries made possible by Project Apollo. The scientific information the astronauts gathered helped scientists explore fundamental questions about the structure of the moon's interior, the composition of its crust, and its formation, transforming our understanding of the moon and early solar system. •

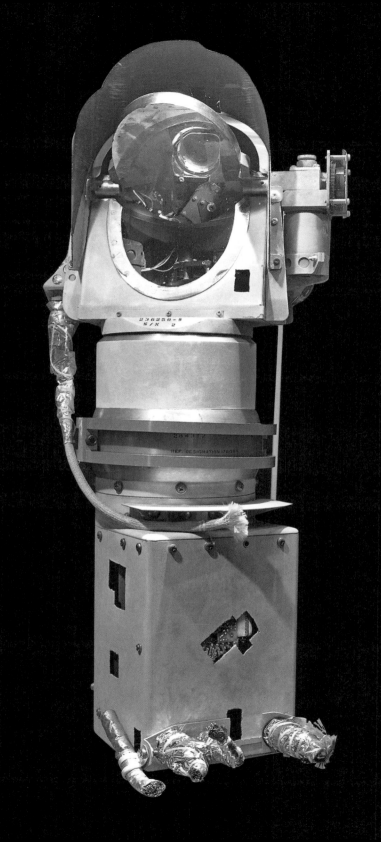

32 Camera, Surveyor 3 Spacecraft

Date: 1967 (recovered 1969)
Manufacturer: Hughes Aircraft Company
Origin: Playa Vista, California
Materials: Stainless steel, anodized aluminum, plastic, rubber, glass
Dimensions: 8 by 16 by 5 inches

This camera, taken off the Surveyor 3 spacecraft by the crew of Apollo 12, has the distinction of being the first—and to this day, only—piece of a robotic spacecraft retrieved and brought back to Earth by a human crew. It is fitting that an Apollo crew brought it back, as it helped to ensure their safe journey to another world.

Before NASA could send humans to the moon, they had to gather information about the conditions humans and their spacecraft would encounter on the lunar surface. Was the ground stable and solid enough to hold a 16-ton vehicle? Was the lunar dust too deep and loosely packed for a human to walk? What hazards existed in the lunar terrain that were not visible from orbit?

From 1966 to 1968, the United States sent seven robotic Surveyor spacecraft to the moon to perform the nation's first soft landings on another world. Five of these spacecraft worked as planned, landing intact and operational. Once there, they used a suite of instruments to perform tests at their landing sites. Back on Earth, scientists and engineers used their findings to design the Apollo lunar module (LM) and to plan scientific and exploratory activities for the astronauts.

Surveyor 3, launched on April 17, 1967, was the second craft to land successfully. It carried this television "survey camera" attached to its frame. Standing roughly as tall as a set of human eyes, the survey camera was able to capture images of the lunar horizon as it would look to a human standing on the moon. The camera's wide-angle mode let it record panoramic images, while its narrow-angle mode took more detailed images containing 10 times as many frames. These smaller images could be "stitched" into mosaic panoramas that contained a wealth of scientific information.

The Surveyor 3 camera sent over 6,000 pictures back to Earth. Most were of the spacecraft's surroundings, but it also captured images of Earth during a solar eclipse, during which it also took a photo of the planet Venus.

In addition, the camera worked with a robotic "surface sampler" arm mounted below it, designed to conduct tests on the mechanical properties of lunar soil. The arm's scoop scraped and dug trenches in the soil that were then photographed by the camera.

On November 19, 1969, two and a half years after Surveyor 3 landed, Apollo 12's LM *Intrepid* touched down within 535 feet of the robotic spacecraft in a demonstration of precision. During

their second excursion outside of the LM in the Oceanus Procellarum (Ocean of Storms), astronauts Alan Bean and Charles "Pete" Conrad walked to the lander and removed the camera to bring with them on their return to Earth.

Bringing parts of Surveyor 3 back from the moon gave NASA scientists an opportunity to analyze the long-term effects of spaceflight on spacecraft materials. In addition to the camera, Bean and Conrad returned with some electrical cables, the sample scoop, and two pieces of aluminum tubing.

Back on Earth, scientists found microscopic craters on the returned pieces, the result of micrometeorite bombardment from its time on the moon. They also found that solar radiation had darkened the painted surfaces of the lander. Some evidence indicated that bacteria carried from Earth to the moon on the unsterilized camera might have survived its time in the harsh lunar environment. Although this finding has since been disputed, it prompted the need for

full sterilization of future robotic missions to planetary surfaces.

In 1976, the Smithsonian National Air and Space Museum (NASM) put the Surveyor 3 camera on display, with material cut away from the camera for analysis. Thirty years later, NASA scientists visited the museum to perform further analysis on the camera to better understand the impact of landing new missions near existing hardware. The camera showed effects of "sandblasting" from the Apollo 12 lunar module rocket exhaust propelling lunar dust toward Surveyor 3. •

33 Apollo Lunar Surface Experiment Package

Date: ca 1971
Manufacturer: Bendix Aerospace Systems
Origin: Houston, Texas
Materials: Steel, Mylar, plastic, Styrofoam, covered metal
Dimensions: 24^7/$_{16}$ by 21^5/$_8$ by 27^9/$_{16}$ inches

Soon after John Young and Charles "Charlie" Duke, Jr., stepped foot on the moon in April 1972, they released the lunar rover and then pulled out the Apollo Lunar Surface Experiment Package, or ALSEP, which contained a series of scientific instruments. The instruments were a crucial part of the data-collection missions of Project Apollo, and they contributed to the lasting scientific legacy of the missions. Apollo 11 carried an Early Apollo Scientific Experiment Package (EASEP), while each subsequent mission included an ALSEP. The astronauts were first tasked with finding a suitable place to set up the system, and then placing the instruments in an array around a central station, which distributed power to them and housed transmitters, receivers, and data processors.

Cables connected the station to the instruments supplying power as well as communications. Next, the astronauts mounted a specialized antenna on top of the station for relaying data collected by the instruments back to Earth. NASA then provided this information to the respective principle investigators of each experiment for analysis. For months before their flight, the Apollo 16 crew trained with their ALSEP. Even though they knew how and where to set up all of the components, they still encountered mishaps in the moon's unfamiliar environment.

After Duke and Young selected an appropriate site in the Descartes

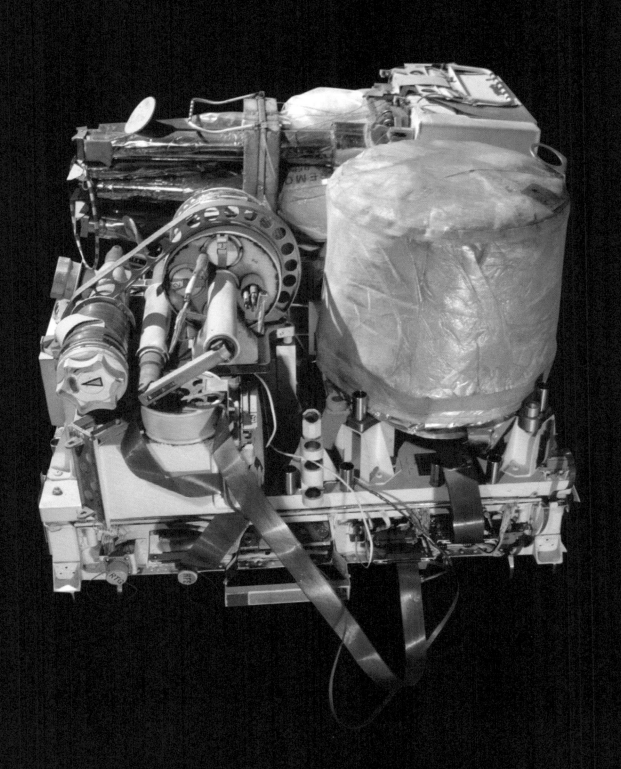

PAGE 199: ALSEPs were stowed in the LM on compact pallets. The Apollo 16 astronauts used this training version to practice deploying the experiments.

Highlands region to deploy the system, Duke put the plutonium fuel rod into the ALSEP's radioactive thermal generator to power all of the experiments. "In training," Duke observed, "we laid it out in a place that was like a big billiard table; and everything went out and you could put it exactly right and get the lines straight. Up on the Moon, it was not that at all, of course, and you had to just do the best you could." Duke then hooked instrument packages to a bar, and "started jogging out to the deployment site," which was a couple hundred meters from their lunar module *Orion*. Duke accidentally dropped a package on the way, but, as he later recalled, "it turned out that the thing was pretty robust."

Even with extensive training, the moon's one-sixth gravity created new challenges for the Apollo 16 crew. As Duke drilled holes for a heat flow experiment, Young began setting up the central station and its connecting cables. As Duke remembers the scene, "it was a spaghetti bowl full of cables around this thing, with all the experiments attached, and—like a spider web." Young caught his foot in one of the cables, pulling out the data source collector and power source for the lunar heat flow experiment, one of the scientific instruments. Duke recalled warning NASA technicians during training that the cables "up on the moon, one-sixth gravity, these things are going to coil up like spaghetti."

And, he observed, "sure enough, that's what happened."

To Duke, the misstep was "tragic because I had worked hard on it, and the principal investigator was a real great guy, and, you know, we wanted to do a good job." He asked Mission Control to tell Mark Langseth, the principal investigator on the experiment and a pioneering Earth scientist at Columbia University, that they were sorry. Fortunately, Young's misstep did not ruin the experiment in the end. Langseth was able to use the data collected from similar equipment deployed by the previous and next missions, Apollo 15 and Apollo 17, to show that there was no evidence of recent volcanic activity and that the moon had already dissipated much of its internal heat.

In addition to the rectangle-shaped heat flow experiment, the Apollo 16 ALSEP held three other experiments. The passive seismic experiment (PSE), enclosed in a white cylinder, was created to measure moonquakes and impacts, which in turn would help determine the physical properties of the lunar crust and interior. Similarly, the active seismic experiment (ASE), to the left of the PSE, used a string of three geophones driven into the ground to record signals generated by controlled explosions—19 shotgun-like explosives fired by Young from different locations around the instrument. After the astronauts left the moon, a remotely operated mortar (the white rectangle at the bottom of the pallet), fired off three more charges that impacted and burst some 1,000 meters away. Finally, the ALSEP held a lunar surface magnetometer, capable of measuring the magnetic field at the lunar surface.

Once the astronauts set up the ALSEP, Mission Control operated the system from Earth. The principle investigators, many of whom were scientists and agencies and universities collaborating with NASA, used the data to answer questions about the lunar environment. The Apollo 16 ALSEP continued to collect data from April 21, 1972, through September 1977, when NASA ended the program. •

34 Carruthers's Far Ultraviolet Camera/ Spectrograph

Date: Late 1960s
Manufacturer: Naval Research
Laboratory
Origin: Washington, D.C.
Materials: Gold-plated metal,
electronics
Dimensions: 16 by 29 by 18 inches

Apollo 16's lunar module (LM) *Orion* landed near the Dollond impact crater in the Descartes Highlands on April 21, 1972, for a 71-hour stay. It was the fifth crewed landing in the Apollo series, and the first to carry a small astronomical telescope. When the astronauts were not roving the countryside, collecting samples and taking pictures, they were setting up a series of scientific experiments to monitor thermal, magnetic, and seismic activity; or examining the properties of the lunar surface; or manually operating a small golden telescope to image and spectrally record Earth's outer atmosphere, bright stars, and the vast spaces between the stars.

Called the Far Ultraviolet Camera/ Spectrograph, it was the creation of George R. Carruthers and his team at the Naval Research Laboratory (NRL) in Washington, D.C. Carruthers had developed a highly sensitive camera system that employed electronographic amplification of the optical signal, and recorded it on special high-sensitivity ultra-fine-grained photographic nuclear-emulsion film. The camera itself was designed as a Schmidt optical system, popular with astronomers to record wide fields of the sky to very faint light levels.

Carruthers embedded the optical system into a magnetic focusing cylinder. Light passed through a weak ultraviolet-transparent corrector lens and onto a very fast three-inch spherical mirror that concentrated the light onto a small convex photocathode. The photocathode

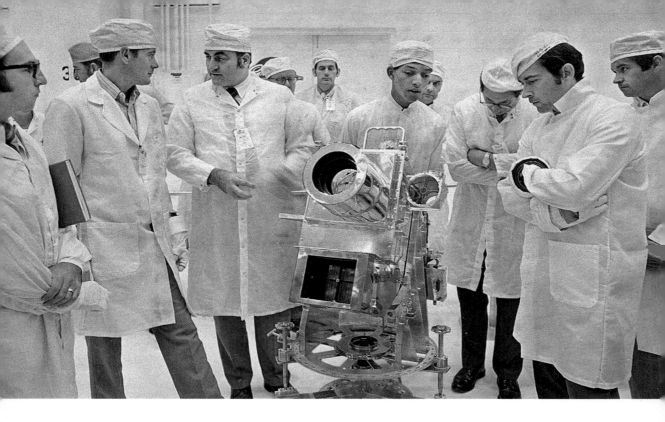

converted the high-energy ultraviolet photons into electrons, which were then accelerated and focused magnetically into an image behind the main mirror where a transport carried the film in a roll strip. Carruthers flew test versions on sounding rockets and proved its worth.

Carruthers's main goal was to get a first glimpse of what the universe looked like in the high-energy far ultraviolet region of the spectrum, which astronomers suspected held many answers to how stars and galaxies form. This was the early space age, and as yet there was little knowledge of this high-energy realm. The NRL group had been a pioneer in the field of far ultraviolet and x-ray astron-

omy, and was especially interested in the distribution of hydrogen in Earth's upper atmosphere, and in the universe. Carruthers was one of the group's rising stars.

Astronauts on the moon could not see anything fainter than Earth in the sky because their eyes had to be protected by dense visors. So Carruthers designed the instrument to be easily handled. He calculated where each of his target fields would be located in the sky at the times the astronauts would use the telescope. All they had to do was set up the camera on its tripod, level and orient it, rotate it in its cradle to predicted altitudes and azimuths, and then make the exposures and advance the film. They also had to manually flip the camera between its two modes: direct imaging and spectroscopy, where the camera was tipped to receive dispersed light from a collimated objective grating.

To keep the camera's temperature stable, the astronauts placed it in the shadow of the LM. However, because Apollo 16's touchdown was 6 hours past its scheduled time, the sun was higher in the sky. This meant the camera had to be closer to the LM, which blocked out almost a fifth of the sky—including several planned targets. During the three extravehicular activities (EVAs), the astronauts photographed some 11 regions of the sky, including Earth. They removed the film transport from the camera in the third EVA and returned it to Earth. Nearly 200 usable frames were recovered, including 85 images and 68 spectra. They captured over 500 stars, some nebulae and galaxies, parts of the Great Cygnus Loop, the North America Nebula, and the Large Magellanic Cloud. In particular, Earth's geocorona—a belt of ionized hydrogen at the outer limit of our exosphere—was spectacular, showing airglow patterns and polar auroras.

The little telescope still sits on the moon in the Descartes Highlands. Only the film transport was returned to Earth. NASA retained various backup units at its Manned Spacecraft Center and at the end of the Apollo era instituted the process of decommissioning hardware, much of it to NASA visitor centers and to the National Air and Space Museum, including the one shown on page 205.

Two engineering models of the lunar camera were transferred to NASM in June 1981. Of the two, the one marked serial number 4 was distinctly more complete. It was loaned to the NRL in 1992 so that Carruthers and his Project SMART students from Washington, D.C., could restore it. As part of the restoration, Carruthers attached the flown film transport mechanism at the back end of the electronographic camera and added other components to make it as real as possible. •

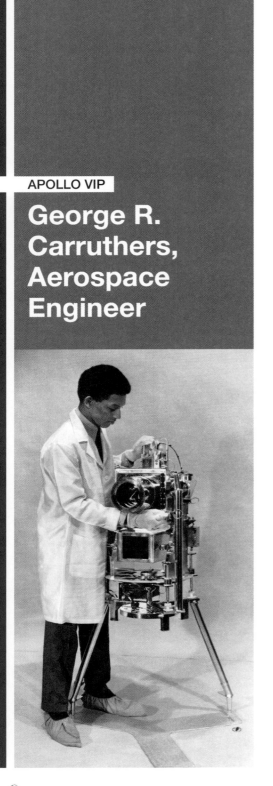

APOLLO VIP

George R. Carruthers, Aerospace Engineer

George Robert Carruthers designed and built the first astronomical telescope that observed the universe from another world: our Earth's moon. Working at the U.S. Naval Research Laboratory (NRL) in Washington, D.C., Carruthers created a highly sophisticated and versatile telescope that could take direct images of the universe as well as analyze its contents. Most of all, the telescope had to be compact, lightweight, and usable for the Apollo 16 astronauts on the lunar surface.

Born in 1939 in Cincinnati, Ohio, Carruthers arrived at the NRL in 1964, armed with a Ph.D. in aeronautical and astronautical engineering from the University of Illinois. He had been building and using telescopes since childhood and was mentored in classes at the Adler Planetarium in Chicago, where the family moved after Carruthers's father died in the early 1950s. In high school, Carruthers read voraciously about rockets, spaceflight, and astronomy. He was particularly fascinated by x-ray astronomer Herbert Friedman and other scientists who were sending detecting devices into space aboard V-2, Viking, and Aerobee rockets.

As soon as he was ready, Carruthers applied for and won an National Science Foundation postdoctoral scholarship to the NRL, eventually becoming a full staff member in Friedman's group within its E. O. Hulburt Center for Space Research. While in graduate school at Illinois, Carruthers was frustrated because he found no mentors willing to let him combine his talents and passions for engineering and astronomy.

Carruthers, once assigned to Talbot Chubb's Upper Air Physics branch, joined an experimental rocket astronomy team to search for molecular hydrogen in space. This required sensitive detectors for the ultraviolet portion of the spectrum. To meet the challenge, Carruthers developed an electronographic camera that amplified images electronically for recording on photographic film. Guided by Chubb and mentored by Julian Holmes at the NRL, he devised especially efficient and reliable electronographic cameras and flew them on rockets in the late 1960s.

In 1969, Carruthers responded to an open NASA "announcement of opportunity" to create experiments for future Apollo flights. He suggested an ultraviolet spectrograph to further explore the nature and distribution of molecular hydrogen in the universe, especially in Earth's outermost atmosphere. Carruthers soon learned that another astronomer, Thornton Page of Wesleyan University, had proposed almost the same thing, using a direct imaging camera. NASA, as it often did, put the two together, and Carruthers designed a single telescope that could take both images and spectra. By the time NASA gave them the green light, Carruthers and his NRL team had less than two years to get it fully ready. When Apollo 16 carried it to the moon, it worked flawlessly.

Carruthers remained at the NRL for the rest of his career, continuing to develop and perfect a wide range of ultraviolet detectors. His devices flew on Skylab, and later on space shuttle missions. In his later years, Carruthers became an avid mentor, inspiring schoolchildren to get practical hands-on experience in his dual worlds of science and engineering.

35 Lunar Rover Wheel

Date: 1970
Manufacturer: GMC AC Electronic Defense Research Laboratories
Origin: Santa Barbara, California
Materials: Wheel: zinc-coated steel piano wire, titanium treads; Fender: epoxy-impregnated fiberglass
Dimensions: Wheel: $9^7/_{16}$ by $31^1/_2$ inches; Fender: $31^1/_8$ by $10^5/_8$ by $17^{11}/_{16}$ inches

"The rover really seemed to be another spacecraft, even though we were operating on the surface of the moon. Every time we'd hit a rock or a bump, we'd just fly into space," recounted James "Jim" Irwin, Apollo 15 lunar module pilot. Irwin and crewmate Dave Scott were the first humans to drive the lunar roving vehicle (LRV) on the moon. Boeing Aerospace designed the LRV to extend the astronauts' range, enabling astronauts to collect lunar sam-ples much farther from their lunar module. With the vehicle, crews could drive for 40 miles at a speed of up to 11 miles an hour, although as Irwin observed, it became bouncy above five miles an hour. The wheel pictured here is a spare from an LRV.

Apollo 15, 16, and 17—called "J" missions—involved longer stays on the moon and more extensive EVAs. These crews spent three days collecting samples, setting up scientific experiments, and evaluating equipment. The LRV, a battery-powered "dune buggy," was tucked into the descent stage of each of the three lunar modules, its wheels and seats collapsed inward to make it more compact during flight. Deployment of the vehicle took roughly 11 minutes, with an additional six minutes for navigational alignment and other checks. Dave Scott compared it to deploying an "elaborate drawbridge."

Boeing produced 11 LRVs in total: eight for use in development and testing and three for the actual Apollo missions.

A subcontractor, General Motors Defense Research Laboratories, designed the wheels. The first operational flight model was ready in March 1970. During testing, engineers subjected the LRVs to extreme conditions, far more severe than anticipated during the lunar missions. Astronaut Charlie Duke collaborated with the LRV development team to make sure the design and placement of handholds would allow for efficient entry and exit.

Powered by a pair of 36-volt batteries, the LRV had a wheelbase of more than

seven feet, a 10-foot chassis, and stood nearly four feet high. During a normal EVA, crews drove for up to three hours, then parked the vehicle for a similar amount of time to allow the batteries to cool. The LRV came with a T-handle joystick, rather than a steering wheel, that directed the vehicle to move forward or backward. Each individual wheel had an independent traction drive motor, allowing for four-wheel steering. The LRVs could handle slopes of up to 25 degrees, clear obstacles up to a foot high, and park safely on slopes of up to 35 degrees.

Because the moon has a very weak magnetic field, astronauts could not rely

Eugene Cernan, commander of Apollo 17, stands next to the lunar rover. The gold camera and antenna in the foreground provided Mission Control with a live television feed to oversee EVAs.

on a compass for navigation. Instead, they used what was called a "dead reckoning" system. After orienting the system's navigational gyroscope to the sun using a sundial-like instrument on the dashboard, the onboard computer could determine the direction and distance of the LM based on the odometer and gyroscope readings. A high-gain antenna relayed communication, and Mission Control operated a television mounted on the LRV, which allowed for real-time guidance from Houston. A low-gain antenna helped with voice commands during travel on the moon.

Engineers constructed the LRV wheels from a hand-woven mesh made of zinc-coated piano wire, which is lighter and more durable than inflated rubber tires. These hollow tires also have the added benefit of being virtually unaffected by extreme temperature fluctuations, unlike car tires on Earth that expand and contract. Each wheel is composed of 800 steel strands, with titanium treads riveted on top of the wire

"Driving the rover was actually more like flying an airplane, albeit with four wheels, than driving a car."

— Dave Scott,
Apollo 15 Astronaut

in a chevron pattern. The treads gave the wheels traction, preventing them from digging into the lunar soil, potentially spinning out of control. Even so, the wheels did sink in, often creating tracks half an inch deep and kicking up trails of dust.

As Scott recalled, "though the rover could turn on a dime and had very good traction and power, the wire-mesh wheels kicked up impressive rooster-tails of dust, which were deflected by large fenders." He continued, "it all made for a ride like a cross between a bucking bronco and a small boat in a heavy swell." •

36 Moon Rocks

Date: 3.3 to 4.4 billion years old
Manufacturer: The universe
Origin: The moon
Materials: Anorthosite: plagioclase feldspar; basalt: iron, magnesium, plagioclase feldspar; Breccia: fragments of other rocks
Mass: Anorthosite: 32.8 grams; Basalt: 64.7 grams; Breccia: 101 grams

Twelve astronauts, over the course of six missions, collected nearly 850 pounds of rocks, pebbles, core samples, dust, and soil from the moon. In total, between 1969 and 1972, Apollo crews returned 2,200 samples from six landing sites. Lunar material and data collected during the Apollo missions, along with the three samples featured opposite, transformed our understanding of the formation of the moon and our solar system. The anorthosite, basalt, and breccia pictured represent three primary types of rocks found on the lunar surface, each adding to our understanding of the moon.

Because the astronauts' bulky white EVA suits constrained their ability to lift their arms high or to bend over, engineers designed tools to help them gather lunar material, including tongs, scoops, rakes, hammers, electric drills, and core tubes that could be pounded 70 centimeters into the surface with 50 hammer blows. On the arms of their suits, the astronauts wore checklists that detailed the sample collection schedule for their mission. When they noticed something of interest that was not part of their preplanned activities, they could consult with a team of geologists on standby at Mission Control and modify their EVA.

Sometimes, astronauts made unapproved stops to collect rocks. This was the case with the basalt pictured here. Apollo 15 astronaut Dave Scott decided to collect this sample of basalt at an

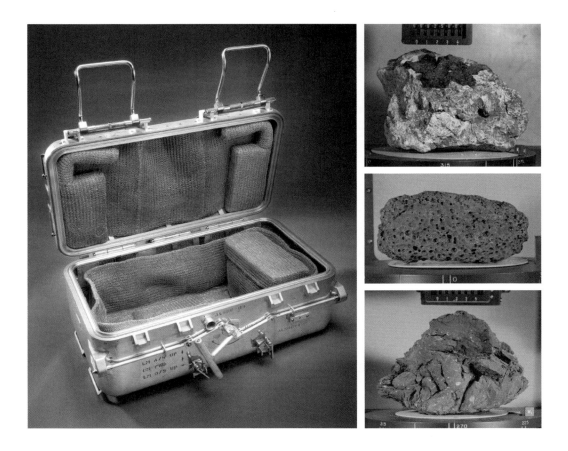

unapproved site. He pretended to fix his rover seat belt while he actually picked up this basalt from the ground. Nicknamed the "seat belt basalt," this specimen, like all basalts, is rich in iron, magnesium, and plagioclase feldspar.

Lunar basalts were formed when hot lava spilled out through cracks in the crust of the moon and flowed over the surface before hardening in the near vacuum of space over hundreds of millions of years. The dark plains on the moon receive their color largely from

basalts. On Earth, basalts are found in volcanic regions such as Hawaii.

The crew also collected breccias, formed when the relentless bombardment of meteorites over the moon's long history broke rocks into smaller fragments and the heat and pressure of these impacts fused some fragments together to create newer composite rocks. Apollo 17 astronauts Eugene Cernan and Harrison Schmitt found the breccia at the rim of a small crater.

Another specimen type, anorthosite, formed from a magma ocean that

covered the moon early in its history. As it cooled and minerals began to form, the heavy ones sank to the bottom and the lighter ones rose to the top. This anorthosite, collected by Apollo 16 astronaut John Young in the Descartes Highlands, is rich with the mineral plagioclase. The thick soil covering the moon, called regolith, is made from pulverized pieces of rock, ground up from years of meteorites bombarding the moon.

The astronauts often photographed the samples in place before they scooped them up, recording the context of the material for later scientific analysis. Alongside the sample they would place a gnomon, a small device that could be used to calibrate the rock's size, color, and orientation. They then placed each sample in a bag with a unique identification number. The astronauts gathered these bags together and placed them in a larger sample collection bag. To carry the rocks back to the lunar module, the astronauts could attach the large sample bags to each other's backpacks or in later missions, the lunar rover. Once back in the spacecraft, they placed the large bags into storage boxes for their return to Earth.

Scientists have determined that moon rocks are chemically similar to Earth rocks, although the Apollo samples have no trace of living organisms and very little water. Based on sample studies, scientists concluded that the early Earth likely endured a glancing blow from a planetary body roughly the size of Mars. Some of the debris ejected into space from this hit amassed, creating our moon. Since the moon's crust formed some 4.4 billion years ago, meteorites have bombarded its surface and lava has flowed between its rocks. Although a roughly equal number of meteorites struck both sides of the moon, its far side appears more cratered than the side facing Earth. This is because much of the near side is covered with relatively young basalt plains, formed from flowing lava that filled many of the large impact basins and craters.

More than scientific specimens, moon rocks have served many roles, from diplomatic gifts to exhibit center-pieces to targets of international crime. By the end of 1970, more than 41 million people attended moon rock exhibits in over a hundred countries. The United States Information Agency (USIA) suggested that these exhibits "brought some of the experience of [the lunar landing] to the home ground of millions." President Richard Nixon sent fragments of moon rocks—one set from Apollo 11 and one from Apollo 17—along with miniature flown flags, to every nation.

Criminals have stolen, smuggled, and sold moon rocks on the black market. In one instance, a stolen rock led to the court case *United States* v. *One Lucite Ball Containing Lunar Material (One Moon Rock) and One Ten Inch by Fourteen Inch Wooden Plaque.*

And a seven-gram moon rock, a gift of the Apollo 11 crew, sits in an air-tight, nitrogen-filled capsule at the center of a stained-glass window at the Washington National Cathedral that has become known as the "Space Window." It commemorates the spiritual and scientific importance of the Apollo program. •

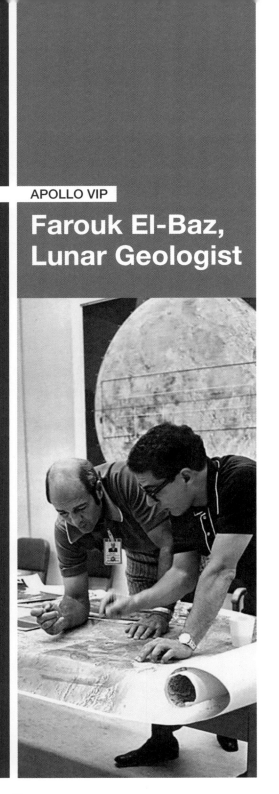

Farouk El-Baz, Lunar Geologist

Farouk El-Baz began his association with Project Apollo at Bellcomm, a NASA contractor advising on lunar science and communications planning. But he did not start his geology career with an eye toward other worlds. Born in Zagazig, Egypt, he pursued his graduate degrees in geology in the United States before teaching mineral studies at the University of Heidelberg in Germany. After a stint at an oil company in Egypt, he applied for a position at Bellcomm, answering an ad looking for geologists to work on Apollo. At Bellcomm he became the supervisor of lunar science planning and operations.

Although El-Baz did not bring a lunar science background with him on his first day on the job, his diligence and insight meant he soon became the person at NASA headquarters who knew the moon like the back of his hand. Providing the first global view of the moon from orbit, the huge Bellcomm Lunar Orbiter program delivered thousands of images of different lunar terrains and structures, which El-Baz took upon himself to orga-

Farouk El-Baz (right) surveys lunar maps with astronaut Ron Evans. El-Baz used his geological expertise to guide the selection of Apollo landing sites and interpret much of the data that came back from the missions.

nize, scrutinizing and characterizing each one.

With his comprehensive knowledge of the lunar surface, El-Baz played an integral role in the landing site selection process. He also coached astronauts on making beneficial visual observations from lunar orbit, and how to locate particular features of interest (or targets of opportunity) designated for study. He won over several reluctant astronauts, awakening in them an interest in the science side of Apollo.

After the last Apollo mission in 1972, with Bellcomm's contract with NASA at an end, El-Baz was recruited by Apollo 11 astronaut Michael Collins, then director of the Smithsonian National Air and Space Museum (NASM). There he established the museum's Center for Earth and Planetary Studies. Today it remains a thriving and respected research group, with geologists active on the science teams of NASA missions to Mercury, Mars, the moon, and more.

During his time at NASM, El-Baz was appointed to the lunar nomenclature task group of the International Astronomical Union (IAU), the organization charged with approving names of craters and other features on planetary bodies. Photography from the Apollo mapping and panoramic cameras formed the basis for detailed topographic photomaps. The features on these maps needed official names, approved by the IAU, so that scientists and others throughout the world could work with a consistent system. El-Baz was instrumental in the construction of these maps and he championed the formal approval of names the astronauts gave to features in their landing sites.

Also while at NASM, El-Baz was principal investigator for Earth observations and photography for the Apollo-Soyuz Test Project, the joint U.S. and Soviet "handshake in space." He also served as science adviser to President Anwar Sadat of Egypt. Currently, as founding director of Boston University's Center for Remote Sensing, he continues his work in orbital science, now directed toward Earth and the study of arid lands.

37 Al Worden's Chronograph, Apollo 15

Date: 1966
Manufacturer: Omega SA
Origin: Switzerland
Materials: Stainless steel, Hesalite (synthetic crystal), brass, jewels
Dimensions: 1 by 1½ by ½ inches

Timing is critical in space exploration. From following detailed checklists to recording the length of engine firings and experiments, precise time kept the astronauts on the schedules meticulously crafted by Mission Control. Command module pilot Alfred "Al" Worden wore the chronograph pictured here (opposite) when he retrieved film canisters from mapping and panoramic cameras in the Apollo 15 service module on the way from the moon back to Earth in the summer of 1971. This was the first deep-space extravehicular activity

(EVA) ever performed in space. The chronograph helped Worden keep time during his risky 38-minute EVA 196,000 miles from Earth.

A chronograph is a type of watch that includes both a display watch as well as a stopwatch. During the Mercury program, in the early 1960s, NASA had yet to research which watch would meet its standards and needs. On the last two missions, Walter Schirra and Gordon Cooper both wore their own watches on board to keep track of time. At the beginning of the Gemini program, Deke Slayton, the chief of the astronaut office, recognized that crews of upcoming missions should be given durable timepieces. James H. Ragan, a young engineer at NASA, determined that the program required manual-winding wrist chronographs that could withstand temperatures from 0°F to 200°F and accelerations up to 12 g. The watches would also need to be waterproof, shockproof, and antimagnetic. Four companies submitted commer-

cially available watches for evaluation. NASA subjected three of these watches to months of rigorous tests.

In the end, the Omega Speedmaster proved reliable and precise, making it the official chronograph of the U.S. civilian space program. It was the only watch that met all requirements as well as the astronauts' approval. First introduced in 1957, the Speedmaster received its name because it included a fixed bezel incremented to measure miles an hour along with the stopwatch. Users could start the chronograph at a marker. After moving a known distance, they would stop the chronograph at a second marker, allowing them to determine

their speed over the distance. The larger third hand on the watch dial is the stopwatch, while three interior dials on the face show a second hand and minute and hour elapsed counters. The fixed bezel is on the outside of the dial.

NASA issued each astronaut their own chronograph roughly six months before their flight so they could become familiar with all of its functions. Unlike the commercially available metal-banded chronographs, the astronauts' versions came with both mesh metal bands and Velcro straps, making it possible to wear in both shirtsleeves and over a pressure suit. Omega sent the first set of 12 Speedmasters to NASA

in October 1964; 20 Speedmaster Professionals followed in July 1966. By 1972, NASA had purchased nearly a hundred Omega chronographs for spaceflight.

In July 1971, Apollo 15 achieved the fourth lunar landing, flew the first scientific instrument module (SIM) bay on an Apollo spacecraft, and conducted the first EVA from a command module in deep space. As planned, Worden climbed out of command module *Endeavour*'s hatch and made three trips to the scientific instrument module bay to retrieve film cassettes from the high-resolution panoramic and mapping cameras, which had imaged roughly 25 percent of the moon's surface at 20-meter resolution.

"It was an unbelievable sensation," he later recalled. "I described it once as going for a swim alongside Moby Dick. There was the CSM [command and service module], all silver white with distinct shadows where equipment got in the way of the sunlight." Because the mapping camera was stuck out in an

> ## "It was the most unbelievable sight one could imagine, and I was so proud of our ability and ingenuity as a nation to do something this magnificent."
> — Al Worden, Apollo 15 command module pilot

extended position, Worden maneuvered around it to pull the panoramic film canister out of the bay. On his second trip, he retrieved the canister from the mapping camera. During his last trip to inspect the cameras, he stopped and took a moment to position himself so that both the moon and Earth were in his field of vision. "I realized," Worden reflected, "that no one in all of history had ever seen this sight before. What an honor it was." Through it all, this chronograph kept precise time. •

Overcoming Catastrophe

Section 8

Introduction

"Failure is not an option . . ."

In the middle of a routine launch rehearsal test a month before the scheduled launch, a wiring defect created a spark in the Apollo Saturn-204 command module capsule, igniting a fire in the pure-oxygen environment. Technicians rushed to the gantry, urgently attempting to open the hatch and rescue the crew, but astronauts Virgil "Gus" Grissom, Ed White, and Roger Chaffee perished inside.

The Apollo 1 tragedy, as it became known, prompted a review board and U.S. Senate investigation. NASA spent more than a year evaluating and redesigning aspects of the spacecraft system. The program stopped using flammable material and completely redesigned the command module's hatch and escape procedures.

Tragedy struck again in 1970, when an explosion in an oxygen tank threatened the safety of the Apollo 13 crew on their way to the moon. A team of flight controllers, spacecraft systems experts, and astronauts banded together to solve problem after problem, ensuring that the astronauts could safely return home. Although lead flight director Gene Kranz did not use the

now famous phrase "failure is not an option" during the mission, it became indelibly linked to him after Ed Harris, the actor playing him in the film *Apollo 13,* uttered the lines. Kranz felt the phrase embodied the attitude of Mission Control so well he used it as the title of his autobiography.

During Project Apollo, NASA managers, scientists, engineers, and astronauts overcame enormous challenges, not only in the development of new technologies but also when they were faced with life-threatening accidents and the high risks of spaceflight. Accidents, both large and small, highlight one of the great legacies of Project Apollo: ingenious problem solving and dedicated teamwork. •

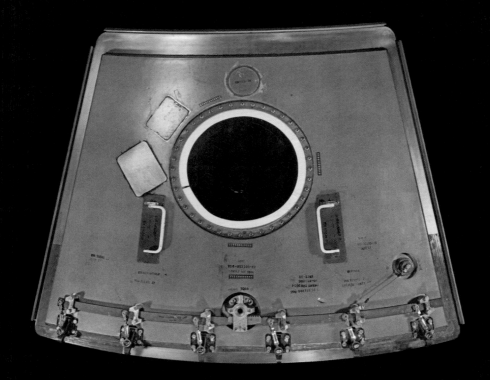
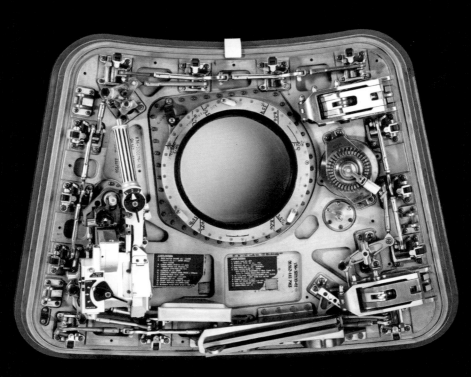

38 Block I Inner Hatch, Apollo 4

Date: 1967
Manufacturer: North American Aviation, Inc.
Origin: Downey, California
Materials: Aluminum, steel, paint, plastic, acrylic (Plexiglas), foam, adhesive, stainless steel, titanium
Dimensions: Approximately 5³/₄ by 42 by 32³/₄ inches

In January 1967, the American space program suffered one of its most crushing setbacks. Three astronauts—Mercury and Gemini veteran Gus Grissom; first American spacewalker Ed White; and Roger Chaffee, planning his first spaceflight—perished as a result of a high-pressure oxygen-fueled fire that broke out in the crew compartment of their Apollo 204 spacecraft, later designated Apollo 1. The accident occurred during a comprehensive test of the entire spacecraft and launch vehicle system on its planned launchpad. The astronauts were preparing to become the first to fly the new three-person Apollo command module into orbit around Earth. After the fire, NASA engineers redesigned components of the spacecraft. The inner hatch (opposite) represents one of the most significant Apollo components modified to ensure the safety of future crews on their way to and from the moon.

The Apollo spacecraft intended for the first crewed Earth-orbital flights were designated Block I. Later spacecraft capable of traveling all the way to the moon were to be Block II. Because the early Apollo missions had no requirement for spacewalks, the mechanisms for ensuring that the crew cabin of the Block I spacecraft was sufficiently well sealed took priority over design for ease of entry and exit through a doorway provided on the side of the spacecraft. Layers of hatches covered the entryway opening: First was the lightweight outer "boost protective cover" designed to protect the spacecraft during the early phases of launch through the atmosphere, then a heat shield that would protect the spacecraft from the intense heat of reentry. Finally came an inner hatch like this one, sealing in the pressure vessel that enclosed and sustained the astronauts.

The investigation that took place following the Apollo fire concluded that "the crew was never capable of effecting emergency egress because of the pressurization before rupture and their loss of consciousness soon after rupture." The report went on to recommend "that the time required for egress of the crew be reduced and the operations necessary for egress be simplified." The review board also identified several aspects of the Block I command module that required redesign. Most apparent was the fact that the astronauts were unable to depressurize the crew compartment and open the hatch before they would succumb to the heat and toxic gases inside. The entire hatch system was changed. Instead of separate hatches, a hinged, outward-opening "unified" hatch was designed for future use. Entirely new procedures and standards were also established to ensure that a repeat of the January 1967 tragedy could never occur.

Meanwhile, the previous Block I command module design was decertified and designated unsafe for crewed flight. But that was not the end of the remaining Block I command modules, or of the removable inner hatches. Several unmanned tests were scheduled using the Block I spacecraft. Command module 017 was assigned to a mission designated Apollo 4, launched on November 9, 1967. Occurring just 10 months after the tragic fire, the Apollo 4 mission was planned to demonstrate the compatibility of the command module and the Saturn V launch vehicle as well as the worthiness of the command module thermal protection system (the heat shield) during atmospheric reentry at speeds approaching that of returning from the moon. The mission was deemed a success. •

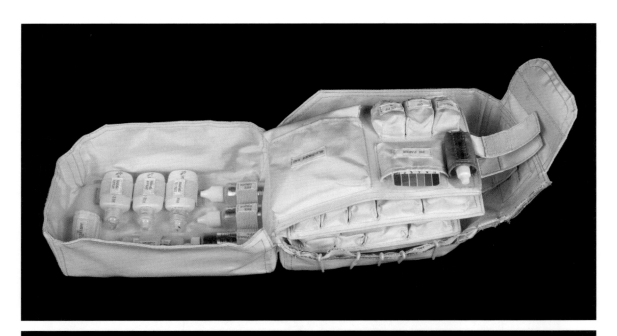

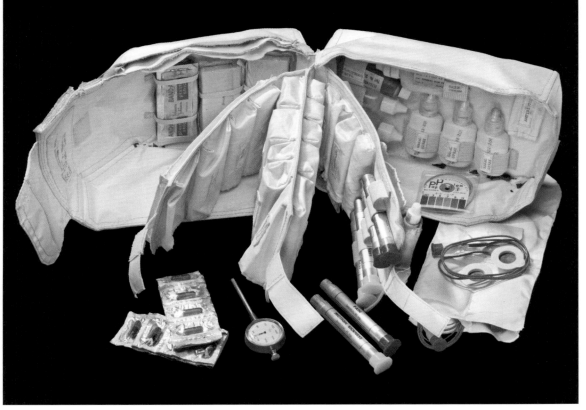

39 Command Module Medical Kit, Apollo 11

Date: 1969
Manufacturer: B. Welson & Co.
Origin: Hartford, Connecticut
Materials: Beta cloth, Velcro, Mylar, other medical goods
Dimensions: 9 by 7 by 6 inches

Every crewed space mission included medical supplies in case of emergency. Most were packed into kits, such as the one stowed aboard the command module *Columbia* during its lunar mission. It contains injectors for motion sickness and pain suppression, a two-ounce bottle of first aid ointment, one-ounce bottles of eyedrops, nasal sprays, both compress and adhesive bandages, an oral thermometer, and an extra crew biomedical harness. Pills in the medical kit included antibiotics, antinauseas, stimulants, painkillers, decongestants, antidiarrheals,

aspirin, and sleeping medicine. What was included in the kit was mainly based on what happened in previous missions, and what medical issues might be likely to occur in flight. The astronauts themselves were given medical training, and their oxygen and carbon dioxide levels were monitored via biosensors.

Years later, this medical kit was selected to be part of an exhibition of artifacts from the Apollo 11 mission. But before it could go on tour, its condition needed to be assessed and its materials and construction documented. Components such as labels, inscriptions, previous repairs, evidence of historical use, material degradation, and any damage were noted to help develop a treatment plan. During background research of this particular item, the conservator discovered information that directed the preservation plan for this important piece of space history.

As part of the initial assessment, two issues were immediately clear: The medical accessory kit was missing the

PAGE 232: Apollo 11's medical kit included basic essentials of first aid as well as added necessities like eyedrops, sleeping aids, and anti-gas pills.

majority of the left side of the lid wall, and the handling strap at the back of the container was completely detached at the right side, and only loosely attached at the left side. The condition issues made it too unstable for transport, but they were also an important part of the history of its usage.

According to the Apollo 11 mission report, when the crew accessed the medical kit during flight, the packaging of many medications and bandages had "blown up like balloons because insufficient air had been evacuated during packaging." The increased volume of the contents prevented the medical kit from closing properly, so they cut away the side wall of the lid to stow the kit. Now that cutaway allows us to see the layered structure of the container, offering greater than normal insight into the object's construction. The walls of the kit are composed of seven layers of various materials, including an outer white Beta cloth shell with five alternating layers of aluminized Mylar and a

synthetic textile, likely Nomex, sandwiched in between. The layered construction helped to insulate the medical supplies from temperature variance and radiation, in addition to protecting it from potential sources of damage such as rips or tears. A similar but more extensive construction was used for the cover layers of the space suits Apollo astronauts wore.

The mission report also described how the container's handling strap detached some time during the flight. Because the damage was part of the mission's story, conservators chose to stabilize the area instead of repairing it to its original condition.

The damaged areas of the Beta cloth container were too unstable for extensive exhibition travel. After consultation with the artifact's curator, the existing loose attachment on the left side was reinforced with navy blue cotton/polyester blend thread, a contrasting color to clearly show what was repair versus original material—and a fix that could

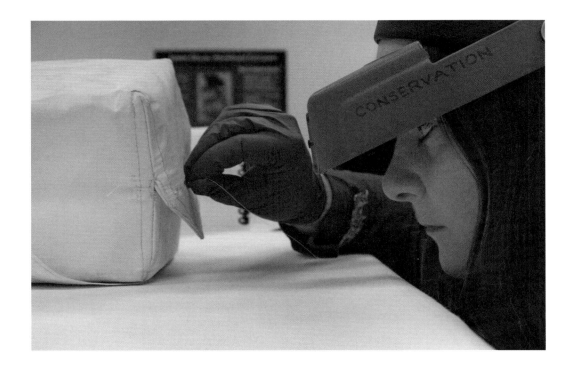

be fully reversible at some future date. This simply anchored the strap along the back of the container.

Stabilizing the cut wall of the medical kit's lid took a more thoughtful approach. Although several options were available, the conservation team chose to use a mount-making solution to keep the area from falling apart. In collaboration with a museum exhibition specialist, the team designed brass clips coated in polyolefin heat shrink tubing that would go over the cut area and hold together the exposed, layered wall of the container. The kit was then ready for transport and display. ●

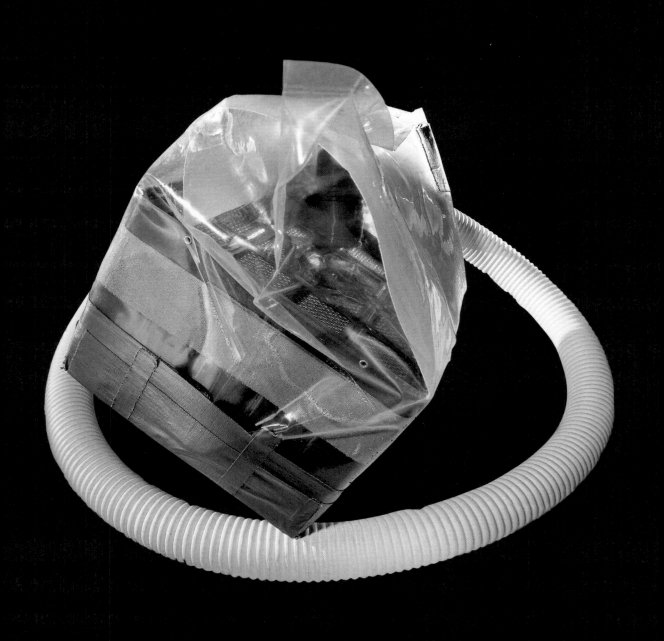

40 Lithium Hydroxide Canister Mock-Up, Apollo 13

Date: 1975
Manufacturer: NASA, Johnson Space Center
Origin: Houston, Texas
Materials: Aluminum, paper, plastic, rubber, cotton, adhesive, paint, lithium hydroxide, carbon
Dimensions: Main body: $7^3/_{10}$ by $7^3/_{10}$ by 9 inches; Hose: 52 by $1^1/_2$ inches

"We're bored to tears down here," quipped capsule communicator—or CAPCOM—Joe Kerwin, 46 hours into the flight of Apollo 13. The first two days of the April 1970 mission had gone smoothly, almost like clockwork. But, within less than 10 hours, Apollo 13 would become one of the most treacher-

ous missions in the history of space exploration. At 55 hours and 55 minutes into the mission, or 9:08 p.m. EST on April 13, command module (CM) pilot John "Jack" Swigert heard a bang and saw a warning light flash on. He radioed, "Houston, we've had a problem here."

Oxygen tank number 2 had exploded. The blast crippled two of three fuel cells and drained oxygen tank 1. Some 200,000 miles from Earth, the Apollo 13 crew had lost the majority of the command module's supply of power and water. This lithium hydroxide canister (opposite) is a mock-up of one of the ingenious solutions that enabled the astronauts to improvise, make unplanned use of whatever was available, and safely return home.

Following the explosion, the Apollo 13 crew immediately shut down the CM systems. They needed to preserve the only remaining power source in the CM—batteries—to steer the spacecraft's brief atmospheric reentry at the end of the mission. Nevertheless, return to Earth

"Yeah, we wish we could send you a kit; it would be kinda like putting a model airplane together or something; as it turns out this contraption is going to look like a mailbox when you get it all put together."

—CAPCOM to Apollo 13 astronauts during the mission, 1970

was still four days away. Without power, the astronauts' survival was in question.

The crew turned their lunar module *Aquarius* into a "lifeboat." But engineers had designed *Aquarius* to support two astronauts for less than three days, not three astronauts for four days. With each exhale, the three men strained the environmental systems of the lunar module (LM). Carbon dioxide quickly began to fill the spacecraft. Although equipped with two lithium hydroxide (LiOH) filters, the LM could not remove the surplus carbon dioxide fast enough. Although the CM also came equipped with LiOH filters, they were not interchangeable with the LM's filters. In a truly unfortunate design decision, the CM filters were box-shaped, made to fit in box-shaped holders, while the LM filters were cylindrical, for cylindrical holders. Hundreds of thousands of miles from Earth, the astronauts faced a challenge: how to fit a square peg into a round hole.

Engineers and astronauts teamed up at Mission Control in Houston to help. Using only the limited supplies that were already available on board Apollo 13—plastic bags, plastic-coated cue cards from a three-ring reference binder, hoses from the lunar space suits, and gray duct tape—they devised the filtration system pictured here and then radioed instructions to the Apollo 13 crew. The jury-rigged contraption worked perfectly. •

41 Eugene Kranz's Vest, Apollo 13

Date: 1970
Manufacturer: Marta Kranz
Location: Houston, Texas
Materials: Fabric, plastic, metal
Dimensions: 22 by 20 inches

"From this day forward, Flight Control will be known by two words: tough and competent," wrote Eugene "Gene" Kranz, deputy of the Flight Control Division and chief of the Flight Control Operations Branch, after the Apollo 1 fire. The loss of astronauts Roger Chaffee, Ed White, and Gus Grissom during a launch rehearsal test on January 27, 1967, rocked Mission Control as it did all divisions at NASA, reinforcing their dedication to "be perfect." Kranz instructed his colleagues to write the words "tough" and "competent" on their blackboards. These words, he told them, should never be erased. "These words are the price of admission to the ranks of Mission Control," he explained. Kranz was wearing this vest (opposite) when Mission Control faced its next major challenge: the explosion of Apollo 13's oxygen tank in flight on April 13, 1971.

When Apollo 13 command module pilot John "Jack" Swigert radioed "Houston, we've had a problem here," Kranz remembered the devastation of the Apollo 1 fire and feared they might lose another crew. Mission Control created the procedures necessary for each Apollo mission. The technical management of vehicles systems—from physiological monitoring to crew activities to recovery support—fell on the Mission Control team. And when something went wrong during a flight, Mission Control needed to find a solution. Once flight controllers realized what had happened to the Apollo 13 spacecraft, the "objective from here on was survival," Kranz recalled. Years later he reflected, "The crew's only hope was Mission Control."

Kranz was the lead flight director on Apollo 13, the third lunar landing

"Failure does not exist in the lexicon of a flight controller."

—Gene Kranz, Apollo 13 lead flight director

attempt. Born in Toledo, Ohio in 1933, Kranz had been fascinated by spaceflight from an early age. After serving in the Air Force and working at McDonnell Aircraft, he responded to NASA's "Help Wanted" advertisement in a 1960 *Aviation Week.* He first worked in the Flight Control Operations Branch at NASA's Langley Research Center before becoming the chief of the Flight Control Operations Branch at the Manned Spacecraft Center in Houston (now the Johnson Space Center).

As he drove to work, Kranz would often play music on the eight-track player in his car—such as John Philip Sousa's "Stars and Stripes Forever"—as a way to build up enthusiasm for the day. Ahead of the Apollo 13 mission, the song "Aquarius/Let the Sun Shine In," from the musical *Hair,* became his new sound track. The Apollo 13 crew had named their lunar module *Aquarius,* and the song's lyrics seemed fitting for the first mission of a new decade. When he pulled into the parking lot to take over the next shift in Mission Control on April 13, the flight could not have been going more smoothly.

By the end of his shift, Kranz and his team were figuring out how to keep the Apollo 13 crew alive. Some plans risked the crew running out of air and water, while others were so fast it was unlikely the crew could live through them. The team worked for the next 40 hours straight to find a solution. Pulled off their normal rotation, this team was also responsible for managing the crew's water and power. Off-duty flight controllers, spacecraft systems experts, and astronauts were eager to help. Eventually, Mission Control devised a plan to have Apollo 13 swing around the moon, giving the spacecraft an extra boost for its return to

Earth. On April 17, 1970, the crew safely splashed down in the Pacific Ocean.

Kranz's wife, Marta, later recalled how, a number of years before Apollo 13, "Gene wanted some kind of symbol for his team to rally around. I suggested a vest." There were multiple Mission Control teams, each assigned a different color. Because Kranz led the white team, Marta sewed white vests for him. Kranz noted that he "started wearing a vest during Gemini 4, and it was an immediate hit . . . from then on, I put on a new vest on the first shift of every mission." The Kranzes found that small details like the vest could build "team cohesion in a high-risk business." Marta's five-button, off-white vest became both an iconic symbol of the white team and Mission Control's tireless efforts to bring the crew home. •

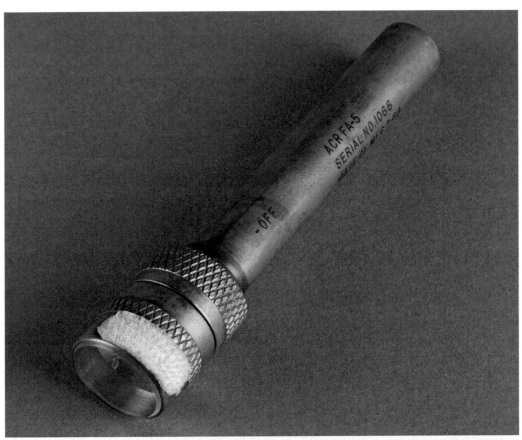

42 Penlight, Apollo 11

Date: 1968
Manufacturer: ACR Electronics
Corporation
Origin: Carle Place, New York
Materials: Brass, glass, Velcro,
plastic, adhesive
Dimensions: 5¼ by 1 inches

After the Apollo 13 crew landed safely back on Earth, they sent a thank-you letter to ACR Electronics Corporation in Carle Place, New York. "The penlight which you have supplied for the Apollo missions has been very useful and dependable in all missions to date," they started. "However," the letter continued, "you deserve special praise for the role it played on our mission—Apollo 13." The mid-flight explosion of an oxygen tank crippled the spacecraft's electrical supply and forced the crew to ration the remainder of the spacecraft's power for vehicle reentry. This had

implications not only for the spacecraft's control and heating but also for the lighting of the cabin. Without overhead illumination, the already complex set of switches became nearly impossible to navigate.

"Your penlights," the crew explained to ACR, "served as our means of 'seeing' to do the job during the many hours of darkness when the sunlight was not coming through the windows." This compact, reliable tool, although far from high-tech, was critical to the astronauts' survival. The crew held the small lights in their mouths "between clenched teeth" as they copied Mission Control's revised procedures. They could beam them into dark corners of the cabin. Even after many hours of use, the flashlights continued to illuminate the spacecraft until the end of the mission.

"Apollo and its success is the result of the dedication, ability, and plain old hard work of thousands of people," the crew reflected in their letter to ACR

"Apollo and its success is the result of the dedication, ability, and plain old hard work of thousands of people."

—Apollo 13 crew

Electronics. "So many in fact, that some we as astronauts sometimes neglect unintentionally." To ensure this was not the case with the small penlights, James Lovell, Jr., Fred Haise, Jr., and John Swigert, Jr., wrote, "Your products and the efforts your personnel expended to make it a good one is appreciated."

The flashlight pictured on page 244 is the same model the Apollo 13 crew referenced in their letter. Apollo 11 astronaut Michael Collins used this particular flashlight during his mission. NASA gave each astronaut their own personal penlight and then stowed additional lights in the spacecraft. Because they were useful even without an accident, they were standard issue equipment for all the missions.

During the Gemini program, ACR constructed some of the penlight's casings out of plastic, but after the Apollo 1 fire, the company started producing them in nonflammable and corrosion-resistant brass. The astronauts activated the lights with a simple twist of the rotating head. A strip of Velcro along the side allowed for secured placement throughout the capsule. Up to five were stored in the CM. Although ACR Electronics penlights had a simple design, they were durable and efficient, two key criteria for Project Apollo.

In December 1981, Lovell wrote about the penlight again, having found it "tucked away in my desk drawer. Not only did it perform on Apollo 13 as our letter stated, but it still works—and the batteries have not been changed since the flight." •

43 Lunar Rover Replacement Fender

Date: 1972
Manufacturer: Eugene Cernan and Harrison Schmitt
Origin: The moon
Materials: Maps, tape
Dimensions: 19$7/8$ by 9$7/16$ by 5$5/16$ inches

"No!" Apollo 17 commander Eugene "Gene" Cernan exclaimed during the last Apollo mission in December 1972. "There goes a fender." In the midst of their first moonwalk, a hammer tucked in Cernan's space suit leg pocket hooked the lunar roving vehicle's right rear fender, accidentally tearing off its extension. "Oh, shoot!" responded his crewmate Harrison "Jack" Schmitt. "I hate to say it," Cernan told Mission Control, "I'm going to have to try to get that fender back on."

They spent around 12 minutes trying to tape the fender extension to the rover. "I'm just going to put a couple of pieces of good old-fashioned American gray tape on it . . . (and) see whether we can't make sure it stays," explained Cernan. But lunar dust immediately collected on the tacky side, preventing the duct tape from sticking. Piece after piece filled with dust. At one point they thought the fender extension was back in place, but it eventually fell off again while driving between experiment sites and was lost on the moon. As soon as Schmitt and Cernan started driving without the extension, the right rear wheel threw up jets of dust, covering them in a cloud of gray lunar material. "I keep getting rained on here," exclaimed Schmitt.

This was not the first fender accident on the moon. During Apollo 15, the crew lost a portion of the left front fender, and the Apollo 16 crew also knocked off their right rear fender extension, suffering a similar cloud of lunar dust. There was so much dust, in fact, that after their

extravehicular activity (EVA), John Young and Charles Duke wrapped their space suit legs in bags, to try and contain the dust before it could clog their suit connectors. But while taking off their suits and placing them in bags, they could not help but dirty their hands, which spread dusty fingerprints around the cabin.

The fender extensions, made of epoxy-impregnated fiberglass, served the essential task of throwing dust as the vehicle moved, instead of onto the rover and astronauts. Not only would a buildup of the dark lunar dust absorb the sun's heat and cause equipment to get hotter, it also contaminated camera lenses, blocked seams, and seemingly clogged every crevice of any moving parts. When the astronauts wiped excess from their visors, the lunar dust—more abrasive than any sand on Earth—could cause scratches and glare. "Oh, boy," Cernan unhappily said, "the thing that makes me sick is losing that fender. I can stand a lot of things, but I sure don't like that."

Engineers at Mission Control were on hand to find a solution. They asked the astronauts for a description of the damage, if it was primarily to the piece that was lost or if there was additional destruction, and then assured them "we'll take a look at it here while you're sleeping." Led by Terry Neal, the Apollo 17 Flight Crew Support Team assessed the equipment and tools that were available to the crew and devised a repair in real time. Apollo 16 astronaut John Young followed the repair procedure on Earth, verifying that the astronauts would be able to carry out the installation steps in their bulky EVA suits.

As the astronauts were eating a breakfast of cold scrambled eggs, Young described the fender procedure to them from Mission Control. "Hey, we spent some time on this fender problem and worked out a pretty simpleminded procedure," Young explained. He instructed them to take four 8-by-10-inch spare pages from the lunar surface maps— essentially stiff, photographic paper—

and tape them together inside the LM to form a roughly 15-by-10.5-inch sheet. They would then take this large sheet to the rover, lay it on top of the fender guide rails, and fasten it, using lamp clamps. It took seven minutes in all, and proved robust enough to last for the remainder of the mission.

Schmitt admired the ingenuity of the support crew, saying, "The guys on the ground had gone out and thought about everything we had in the spacecraft, looked at the inventory, and then, as a team, tried to figure out what in the world we could do to solve the problem using what we had."

At the end of the last EVA, Cernan broke off the remaining three fenders and map-made replacement, packed them onto the LM, and brought them back to Earth. He observed, "Imagine, a little thing like knocking a Rover fender off having the potential of compromising the rest of our mission . . . I knew that we had to find a fix; but I was also confident that we'd find one." ●

Nixon's Speech

Ahead of the Apollo 11 mission, astronaut and White House liaison Frank Borman approached President Richard Nixon's speechwriter William Safire about the potential political repercussions of an accident. "You'll want to consider an alternative posture for the president in the event of mishaps," Borman urged. In response, Safire composed a somber but uplifting message for Nixon to share with the world in the event that Neil Armstrong and Buzz Aldrin were left stranded on the moon.

This memo features a speech President Nixon would have given if the Apollo 11 crew were unable to leave the lunar surface and were left trapped on the moon.

To   :   H. R. Haldeman

From: Bill Safire   July 18, 1969.

IN EVENT OF MOON DISASTER:

     Fate has ordained that the men who went to the moon to explore in peace will stay on the moon to rest in peace.

     These brave men, Neil Armstrong and Edwin Aldrin, know that there is no hope for their recovery. But they also know that there is hope for mankind in their sacrifice.

     These two men are laying down their lives in mankind's most noble goal: the search for truth and understanding.

     They will be mourned by their families and friends; they will be mourned by their nation; they will be mourned by the people of the world; they will be mourned by a Mother Earth that dared send two of her sons into the unknown.

     In their exploration, they stirred the people of the world to feel as one; in their sacrifice, they bind more tightly the brotherhood of man.

     In ancient days, men looked at stars and saw their heroes in the constellations. In modern times, we do much the same, but our heroes are epic men of flesh and blood.

-2-

     Others will follow, and surely find their way home. Man's search will not be denied. But these men were the first, and they will remain the foremost in our hearts.

     For every human being who looks up at the moon in the nights to come will know that there is some corner of another world that is forever mankind.

PRIOR TO THE PRESIDENT'S STATEMENT:

     The President should telephone each of the widows-to-be.

AFTER THE PRESIDENT'S STATEMENT, AT THE POINT WHEN NASA ENDS COMMUNICATIONS WITH THE MEN:

     A clergyman should adopt the same procedure as a burial at sea, commending their souls to "the deepest of the deep," concluding with the Lord's Prayer.

After the Apollo 13 crew returned safely back to Earth, President Richard Nixon flew to Hawaii to welcome home astronauts Fred Haise, James Lovell, and John Swigert (from left to right) and award them the Presidential Medal of Freedom.

Return to Earth

Section 9

Introduction

"Nice ocean you've got here, planet Earth . . . "

Years after his command module *Columbia* splashed down in the Pacific, Apollo 11 astronaut Mike Collins recalled, "I can remember the beautiful water. We were out in the deep ocean in the Pacific. It was such a startling violet color. I remember looking at the ocean and admiring: 'Nice ocean you've got here, planet Earth.'"

Beyond moon rocks, many of the Apollo astronauts brought back a deeper appreciation for their home planet. As some of the first humans to leave Earth, seeing their home from space had a profound impact on their worldviews. After they landed in the violet Pacific waters, they shared their new perspectives and experiences with people around the world.

On a diplomatic tour the Apollo 11 crew took after their flight, Collins told Queen Elizabeth and others gathered at Buckingham Palace that he would like to "take all the world's political leaders up about 100,000 miles, tell them to look back and see how there are no borders and how small the differences between nations really are."

The story of the astronauts' return to planet Earth includes developments in landing and recovery and postflight quarantine, of course. But a large part of the space program's long-term impact came from the diplomatic efforts of the astronauts, the contribution of international partners to the U.S. space program, and the enthusiasm for Project Apollo shared by billions around the globe. •

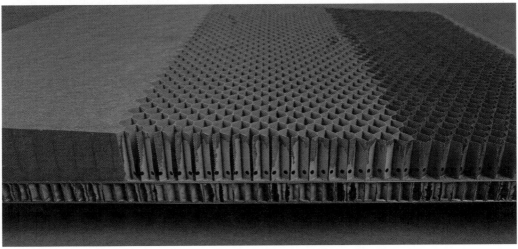

44 Apollo Heat Shield Manufacturing Model

Date: 1975
Manufacturer: Avco Corporation
Origin: Wilmington, Massachusetts
Material: Stainless steel, fiberglass, phenolic resin, various coatings
Dimensions: 18 by 2½ by 48 inches

"There is no turning back now," Apollo 8 astronaut Bill Anders told his crewmates as they began their reentry on December 27, 1968. Soon they noticed a haze outside their windows. Anders and astronaut Jim Lovell first thought it might be sunrise, but they quickly realized it was the glow of ionized gas enveloping the spacecraft. "This is going to be a real ride. Hang on," instructed commander Frank Borman. As the command module plowed through Earth's atmosphere at 25,000 miles an hour, frictional heat started to reach 5000°F. The command module's innovative heat shield protected its human cargo by shedding this extreme heat with an ablative material made from a mixture of resins, fibers, and fillers.

There are three approaches to thermal protection in spaceflight reentry: passive, semi-passive, and active. For Projects Mercury, Gemini, and Apollo, NASA looked to a semi-passive system based on the concept of ablation, in which material decomposes into gas as it becomes hot. As the ablative material vaporizes, it carries the heat away from the capsule. The difficulty with this method is that the ablative material is burned up during reentry. In the 1960s, no known alloy could withstand the intense heat of reentry while still being lightweight enough to be practical for launching into space. Although NASA chose a chemically constructed ablative material, early Soviet vehicles used oak wood.

PAGE 260: A manufacturer's model shows the seven layers of material that made up the heat shield. The layers serve different functions to protect the capsule from high heat and pressure.

OPPOSITE: Engineers begin to apply layers of the command module heat shield.

PAGES 264–265: Astronaut Bill Anders took this photograph, called "Earthrise," during Apollo 8. In one of his last acts as president, Lyndon Johnson sent farewell letters to leaders of every nation in the world with a copy of the image tucked inside.

Ablative material covered the entire command module's outer stainless steel shell, except the windows and exhaust ports. Made up of a fiberglass honeycomb impregnated with a phenolic resin bonded with epoxy-based adhesive, the ablative structure varied in thickness from roughly three inches to less than half an inch. After technicians filled all the honeycomb cells with the sticky puttylike substance, the command module was x-rayed to make sure there were no holes, voids, or defects in the structure. If it passed, the shield would be cured and x-rayed again.

The blunt body of the spacecraft ensured that it would start slowing down early, in the upper atmosphere, limiting the intensity of frictional heat. Although vehicles with slender, more pointed bodies glide easily through the upper atmosphere, they eventually reach higher temperatures because most of their deceleration happens in the thick lower atmosphere. Blunt-bodied and narrow craft experience a similar total heat load, but the bell-like shape of the Apollo command module meant that the capsule would endure a lower temperature heat, even if for a more extended period. Developing material to cope with lower temperature would prove less challenging for engineers, even if just slightly.

The temperatures at reentry became so hot that atoms were stripped of their electrons. Glowing plasma engulfed the capsules. The light the Apollo 8 astronauts observed was even brighter than for earlier Gemini and Mercury missions because their capsules, returning from the moon, hit the atmosphere at a higher speed. Often described as an intense white, the plasma caused some astronauts to shield their eyes. As the thicker and thicker atmosphere slowed the spacecraft, the astronauts were pushed down in their couches with a force of up to 6 g's. After days of living with weightlessness, this pressure likely felt even stronger to the crew. From Earth, the Apollo capsules looked like shooting stars.

The model pictured at the top of page 260 displays the production stages of the heat shield. First, at left, is the stainless steel plate with a honeycomb substrate material. Next is an adhesive, followed by an unprimed fiberglass honeycomb, a primed honeycomb, and a honeycomb filled cell by cell with uncured phenolic resin. Next we see the cured ablator, sealant, and finally a thermal coating. Avco Corporation, the subcontractor of NASA command module contractor North American Aviation Company, developed, designed, tested, and fabricated the Apollo heat shields. They gave this manufacturing model, along with a sample of a heat shield, to the Smithsonian Institution in 1975. •

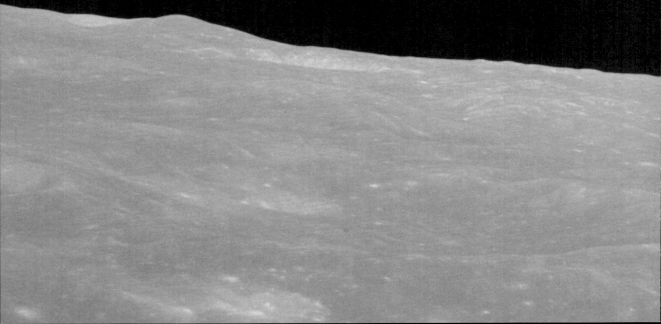

45 Main Parachute, Apollo 16

Date: October 1971
Manufacturer: Northrop Ventura
Origin: Newbury Park, California
Materials: Nylon, aluminum, synthetic fabric, steel, plastic, brass
Dimensions: 903³/₁₆ inches diameter

American engineers designed their spacecraft to land in the ocean. Although water landings were safer, softer, and allowed for a greater reentry window than ground landings, slowing the capsule down still proved challenging, even with the aid of highly engineered parachutes. As Apollo 17 astronaut Ron Evans reported, "the contact with the water is a pretty good smash." Apollo 11 astronaut Mike Collins agreed, remembering, "Splat! Like a ton of bricks we hit."

During early landing testing for Project Mercury, parachutes often experienced what engineers call "squidding." This occurred when the thin atmosphere at high altitude prevented the parachutes from unfurling fully, giving them the appearance of slim squids instead of domes. NASA solved this problem by first stabilizing and slowing the craft with drogue chutes, and then deploying a set of three main ribbon ring-sail parachutes. The latter, developed by Northrop engineer Theodor W. Knacke, had a hole at the center and were made of ribbons fastened together instead of solid fabric. This design allowed air to escape through the gaps of the chutes, creating greater stability at high speeds. Project Gemini used the same system, although some engineers within NASA advocated for an inflatable paraglider landing.

North American Rockwell, in collaboration with Northrop and NASA, developed the Project Apollo parachute system. Although NASA contracted firms to investigate other landing approaches—including a steerable land

PAGE 267: Three 85-foot-diameter parachutes slow Apollo 16's descent into the Pacific Ocean. The small pilot parachutes that helped deploy them are still open.

BELOW: One of Apollo 16's main parachutes. The gaps in the ribbon ring-sail parachute gave greater stability at high speeds.

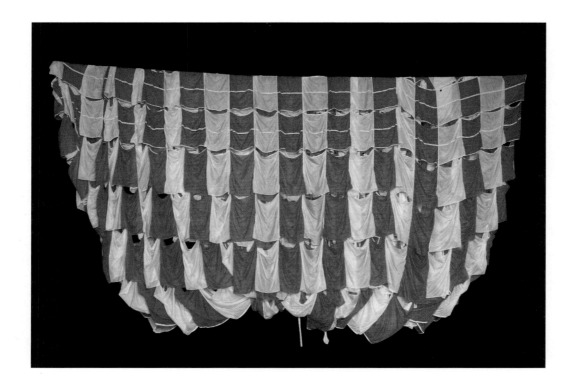

landing—water splashdowns remained the most practical option given the time frame and broader context of the program. Drawing on experience during Mercury and Gemini, engineers created a fully redundant system as a backup, in hopes of ensuring the astronauts' safety in both "regular" and emergency situations. If one of the three main parachutes did not deploy, for example, the remaining two would still be able to slow the command module to a survivable 25 miles an hour. This contingency plan was put into action in 1971 during the reentry of Apollo 15, when one chute deflated because of fuel escaping from the reaction control system.

Speeding back from the moon, the Apollo 16 command module *Casper* landed safely in the Pacific Ocean, thanks in part to its huge, multipart parachute (opposite). As planned, at roughly 24,000 feet, two ribbon drogue parachutes 16.5 feet in diameter provided the initial deceleration and stabilization of the craft. Next, at about 10,000 feet, the drogue chutes were released and small pilot parachutes deployed and released the three main parachutes.

The drag created by these parachutes slowed the capsule from a neck-breaking 175 miles an hour to a much more gentle 22 miles an hour. The main parachutes held the spacecraft at a 27.5-degree angle, ensuring that the command module's slanted corner hit the water first. This configuration was designed to reduce the force of the landing. The main parachutes were then

"A small jerk, and there they are! God, they are a sight to behold, huge orange-and-white blobs . . . bundled together in a reassuring triad. We can survive a water landing with only two good ones, but three looks oh so much better!"

—Michael Collins,
Apollo 11 astronaut

disconnected from the capsule. If the small craft rolled over, leaving the astronauts upside down, crew-deployed flotation bags in the nose would right the craft before recovery swimmers arrived to assist the astronauts out of the capsule. •

46 Mobile Quarantine Facility, Apollo 11

Years: 1967 to 1969
Manufacturer: Airstream, Inc. (sub-contractor), Melpar Corporation (contractor)
Origin: Jackson Center, Ohio; Falls Church, Virginia
Material: Aluminum, glass
Dimensions: 8 feet 7 inches tall by 9 feet wide by 35 feet long
Weight: 12,499⁹/₁₀ pounds

Five years before the first lunar landing, scientists gathered at the National Academy of Sciences to debate the "potential hazards of back contamination from the planets." Would the astronauts bring back deadly lunar microbes from their moon missions? To combat the introduction of possible plague or worse, NASA developed a Lunar Receiving Laboratory (LRL) at the Manned Spacecraft Center in Houston, Texas. The LRL held living quarters, medical facilities, and areas for lunar material to be opened and studied in isolation. But the astronauts were to land in the Pacific Ocean, thousands of miles from the LRL. Melpar Corporation was called upon to solve this problem and develop a Mobile Quarantine Facility (MQF).

According to the NASA contract, the MQF had to be watertight and airtight, as well as equipped with everything required for six people to live in relative comfort for up to five days. It also had to be transportable by ship, plane, and on land. Given the short time frame of the project, and to keep costs down, Melpar purchased commercially available Airstream trailers adapted to meet NASA's requirements. Art Costello, president of Airstream, was enthusiastic: "Ordinarily we expect many benefits to be spun off the space program . . . But this time, we were able to give the space

program something from an earth-bound consumer product."

In June 1967, Airstream sent four vacation trailers from their factory in Jackson Center, Ohio, to Melpar in Falls Church, Virginia. They included many of the standard features—showers, sinks, mirrors—but were mounted on special bases without wheels. Melpar installed exhaust fans and filters to lower the air pressure inside the trailers, one of a number of measures taken to ensure that nothing larger than one-half a micron (roughly two-thousandths the thickness of a dime) could escape.

Since the MQFs would be moved and lifted, their substructure was made out of extruded aluminum, giving them structural rigidity. Melpar provided four MQFs—as well as 35 transfer tunnels and 90 containers for isolating biological material—to NASA just weeks before Apollo 11 launched from Cape Canaveral. The total cost for the four modified Airstreams came to $250,000.

After *Columbia*'s splashdown, biological isolation garments were tossed through the opened hatch on the command module. Once the crew put them on, and before being picked up by helicopter, a specially suited rescue swimmer scrubbed them down with disinfectant. The helicopter crew also donned the suits. When the helicopter and crew aboard landed on the U.S.S. *Hornet* aircraft carrier, the MQF was waiting for them with NASA flight

PAGE 271: Apollo's mobile quarantine facility was a modified Airstream trailer. It is now on display at the National Air and Space Museum Udvar-Hazy Center.

BELOW: Apollo 11 crew (from left to right) Michael Collins, Buzz Aldrin, and Neil Armstrong catch up with world news inside the Mobile Quarantine Facility aboard the U.S.S. *Hornet* shortly after splashdown.

surgeon William Carpentier and a mechanical engineer, John K. Hirasaki, already inside. The crew took showers for the first time in eight days and changed into clean flight suits, with all of the wastewater from the showers stored in isolation containers. They then spoke to President Richard Nixon through a microphone before feasting on steaks and martinis.

Once the U.S.S. *Hornet* arrived at Pearl Harbor in Hawaii, the MQF was off-loaded by crane onto a truck and driven to Hickam Air Force Base. From there it was transferred to a cargo aircraft, with the astronauts still inside. The MQF was outfitted with airplane seats—including seat belts—to keep the crew safe during the flight. After landing at Ellington Air Force Base in Texas, the MQF was moved by truck to the LRL at Manned Spacecraft Center.

The astronauts' wives—one in a white dress, another in a blue dress, and the third in red—met the still sealed MQF in Houston. After 88 hours, the Apollo 11 crew finished their quarantine in the cramped MQF. Two weeks later, NASA scientists were confident that the astronauts had not carried deadly lunar microbes back to Earth. Hirasaki, who joined the astronauts for the entire quarantine, joked "some people call me a lunatic, but that wasn't anything I caught."

The Airstream Travel Trailer Club awarded the astronauts honorary lifetime memberships, and the president of Airstream offered them the use of trail-

> **"The possibility of extraterrestrial life entails the chance that organisms might be returned to earth with returning space missions."**
>
> —Conference on Potential Hazards of Back Contamination from the Planets, July 29–30, 1964

ers and towing vehicles "for travel as you please anywhere on Earth."

The crews of Apollo 12 and Apollo 14 spent time in MQFs as well (because Apollo 13's moon landing was aborted, the crew was not quarantined after their flight). By the Apollo 15 mission in July 1971, the potential of lunar pathogens was no longer seen as a threat, and biological isolation in MQFs was abandoned. •

The Armstrong Purse, Apollo 11

Date: 1969
Manufacturer: NASA
Origin: United States
Materials: Beta cloth, plastic
Dimensions: 10½ by 8 by
12½ inches

In August 2012, the staff at the National Air and Space Museum (NASM)—and people elsewhere around the world—were saddened to learn of the death of Neil Alden Armstrong, the first man to set foot on the moon. Soon afterward, Armstrong's family contacted the museum about items found in his home office. Arrangements had already been made for his papers to be deposited with the archives of Purdue University, his alma mater, but what to do with artifacts and other objects was still to be decided. Along with two colleagues, Allan Needell, museum curator at NASM, traveled to Ohio to assist in inventorying and evaluating the materials. What they found was primarily a collection of medals and awards, models, and small pieces of equipment and clothing. They offered help in determining what items might have special historical significance and require special resources for preservation and display.

A few weeks later, Needell received an email from Carol Armstrong, Neil's widow. In one of their closets, she had found a white cloth bag filled with assorted pieces that looked like they may have come from a spacecraft. She wanted to know if they were also of interest to the museum, and included a photograph of the bag and its contents, spread out on her carpet.

The bag itself was immediately recognizable. It was what the astronauts called a "McDivitt purse," so named for the way it opens and closes, like a clutch purse. Apparently Apollo 9 commander James McDivitt first suggested the need for such a bag to temporarily stow items

Neil Armstrong carried this collection of clamps, cords, a camera, and other pieces of equipment home in a Temporary Stowage Bag, or "McDivitt purse."

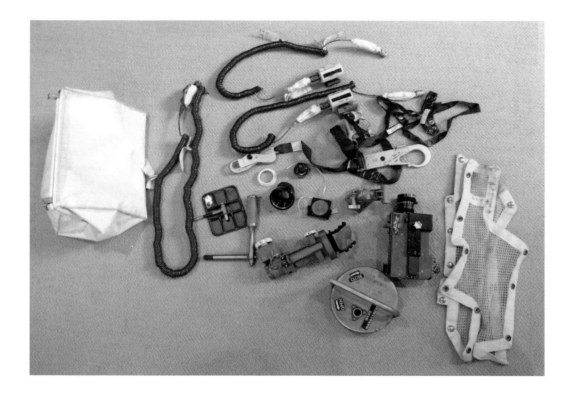

when there was not enough time to return them to fixed stowage locations. Officially called a Temporary Stowage Bag, or TSB, the purse was stowed in the lunar module during launch with pins that fit into sockets in front of the commander's station, to the left of the spacecraft's hatch.

This time, in addition to members of his museum staff, Needell gathered as part of his team some experts who collaborated on the Apollo Lunar Surface Journal (ALSJ) website, an indispensable cache of detailed information about all aspects of the Apollo program. Their goal was to confirm if any or all of these items had actually flown in the lunar module *Eagle* during the historic Apollo 11 mission. The team began with a close examination of

"To those of you out there on the network who made all of the electrons go to the right places, at the right time—and not only during Apollo 11—I would like to say thank you."

—Neil Armstrong at Goddard to tracking network personnel, March 18, 1972

Armstrong's TSB and its contents, not only checking part and serial numbers and other physical evidence but also listening to contemporaneously recorded conversations between the astronauts and Mission Control. On these they heard, soon after Armstrong and Buzz Aldrin rejoined Michael Collins in the command module in lunar orbit, Armstrong saying: "You know, that—that one's just a bunch of trash that we want to take back—LM parts, odds and ends, and it won't stay closed by itself. We'll have to figure something out for it." The Apollo 11 crew later described to Mission Control the same "odds and ends" container as filled with "10 pounds of LM miscellaneous equipment." It was important that the amount and distribution of any added weight on *Columbia* be carefully recorded, so that the return trajectory and reentry parameters could be calculated with precision.

After that, with more hard work, the museum team was able to determine with almost complete certainty that every one of the items was indeed from the lunar module *Eagle.* Armstrong's "purse" and all of the items in it are now carefully preserved as part of the Smithsonian National Air and Space Museum collection. Each piece may well help tell a story about the first human trip to another world and what artifacts meant to at least one of the participants. For

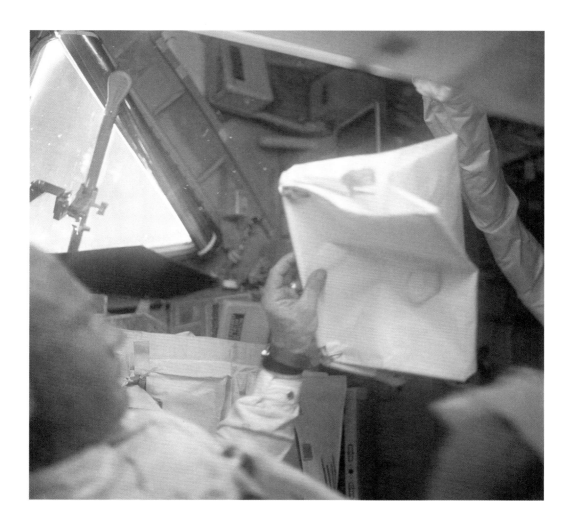

example, among the items selected for return was one of two waist tethers designed to secure astronauts should they have to spacewalk from the lunar module back to the command module if there was a problem reconnecting the two space-craft in orbit around the moon. Followers of the Apollo missions have long been familiar with the story of how Neil Arm-strong, when on the lunar surface, used one of the waist tethers to rig a way to support his feet during the single rest period on the moon. Telltale remnants of the paint used inside the lunar module confirms that this tether was the one that served that improvised function. Because he stashed it in his purse, Armstrong ensured that this artifact, along with many others, brings alive a story that, until now, has been illustrated only by technical debriefings dictated by the astronauts after arriving home. •

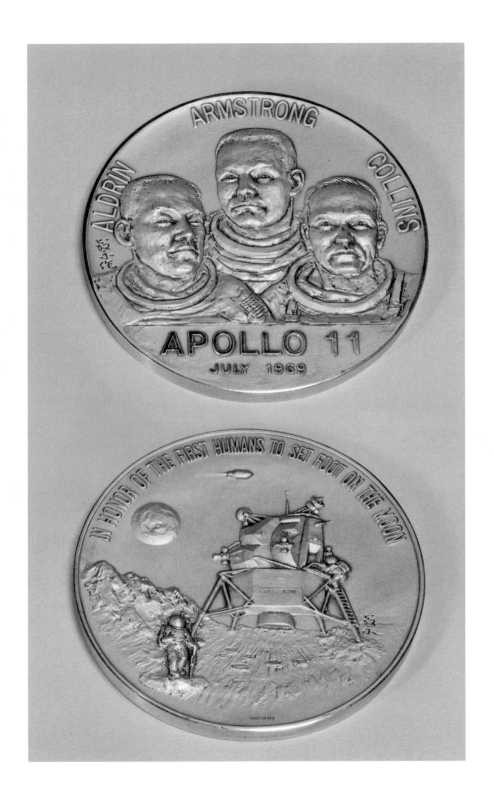

48 Neil Armstrong's World Tour Medal, Apollo 11

Date: ca 1969
Manufacturer: Matsumoto Kisho Industries
Origin: Japan
Material: Silver
Dimensions: 4 inches

As the Apollo 11 crew's motorcade drove through the streets of Tokyo in November 1969, thousands of onlookers showered them in confetti, waved Japanese and American flags, and shouted the traditional cheer: "Banzai—may you live 10,000 years." This was the last stop on a worldwide goodwill tour the Apollo 11 crew undertook at President Richard Nixon's request. During this "Giant Step" tour in the fall of 1969, the astronauts and their wives, along with a large support staff, visited more than 20 countries. In Tokyo, Neil Armstrong, Buzz Aldrin, and Mike Collins met with Prime Minister Eisaku Sato, who pinned Japan's cultural medals on the astronauts' lapels, the first time foreigners received this honor. Emperor Hirohito, whom the U.S. State Department had identified as a space exploration enthusiast, later welcomed the astronauts and their wives at the Imperial Palace. This commemorative silver medal (opposite), minted by Matsumoto Kisho Industries, was likely given to astronaut Neil Armstrong during this visit to Japan.

Since the beginning of the space age, the U.S.S.R. and the United States had invested heavily in promoting their space accomplishments in Japan, in particular. In the Cold War contest for global political alignment, American and Soviet politicians often viewed Japan—as U.S. Secretary of State John Foster Dulles once put it—as "the linchpin of the future Asian economy." After Yuri Gagarin became the first

"The Japanese follow our program as though it were their own."

—John Glenn, Mercury astronaut, to President Richard Nixon

human in space in April 1961, he visited Japan on an international goodwill tour. The following year, when John Glenn became the first American to orbit Earth, the United States exhibited his space capsule Friendship 7 in Tokyo. It attracted more than 12,000 people within hours and, in just four days, more than half a million people visited the exhibit. A year later, when Glenn visited Japan in person with his family, the American ambassador to Japan, Edwin O. Reischauer, enthused that they "were [an] effective demonstration of typical American virtues," and that "many seemed, for [the] first time, to appreciate [the] openness of the U.S.

space program as compared to [the] Russian [program]."

Leading up to the first lunar landing, nearly a million people visited 36 Apollo 11 exhibits scattered throughout Japan. More than one in eight of the foreign correspondents at the Apollo 11 launch in Cape Canaveral were Japanese. An estimated 90 percent of Japanese people watched television coverage of the flight, one of the highest levels of interest of any country in the world. During the mission, the U.S. Embassy in Tokyo received an outpouring of gifts, from paper cranes given for good luck to original artwork to letters of good wishes. When the United States put a large moon rock collected by the Apollo 12 crew on display at Expo '70 in Osaka, it drew a total crowd of roughly 18 million people.

Armstrong visited Japan again in August 1971. Speaking to 23,000 Boy Scouts from 90 countries at the Boy Scout Jamboree at the foot of Mount Fuji, Armstrong stressed that space and

scouting share the same aim: fostering understanding and cooperation among all people in all nations on the planet. Armstrong shared this message in many places he visited around the world following Apollo 11. When speaking at a 1969 USO tour stop in Bangkok, for instance, a soldier asked, "I wanna know why the U.S. is so interested in the moon instead of the conflict in Vietnam." Armstrong responded, "That's a great question . . . one of the advantages of the space activity is that it has promoted international understanding and enabled cooperative effort between countries on many levels and will continue to do so in the future." The medal shown here is just one material example of the connections between Project Apollo and international relations. •

Simon "Si" Bourgin, United States Information Agency Science Adviser

Almost immediately after the Apollo 11 crew returned from the moon in July 1969, President Richard Nixon became anxious that they begin a worldwide diplomatic tour. Recognizing the foreign relations advantages of such a tour, Nixon urged his most trusted advisers, including Henry Kissinger, Peter Flanigan, and H. R. Haldeman, to take a hands-on role in planning. Space accomplishments, as Nixon and previous presidents appreciated, could be an influential source of U.S. policy support abroad. In the fall of 1969, the crew visited major cities on each continent on a presidential goodwill tour named "Giant Step." Simon Bourgin, or "Si" to his friends—astronauts included—helped them navigate local politics.

The Apollo astronauts not only relied on Bourgin's country briefings ahead of their diplomatic appearances, but they also trusted his guidance on the public relations dimensions of spaceflight. The son of Jewish immigrants from Russia, Bourgin was born in a small town at the edge of the Boundary Waters, an expanse of wilderness straddling Minnesota and Ontario. Entirely by coincidence, the Apollo 15 crew visited Bourgin's hometown in October 1970, during their training. Ely, Minnesota, boasted a rare greenstone called Pillow Rock, chemically similar to moon rocks.

After receiving a degree in political science and economics from the University of Chicago, Bourgin traveled to Washington, D.C., then Europe to cover World War II as a journalist. In the 1950s, he moved to California to write for *Newsweek.* When Edward R. Murrow recruited him to the USIA, he excitedly took to working with the Apollo crews. "After the narcissism of many of the denizens of Hollywood," he reflected, "these men were true superstars."

At the USIA, Bourgin recalled, "one of my first jobs was to escort [the astronauts] as they made diplomatic tours around the world, visiting various foreign missions as they exported the kind of American optimism and heroism and technological sophistication for which we were justifiably known." He became close with Frank Borman, commander of Apollo 8 and later NASA's White House liaison. A few days before his flight,

Borman called Bourgin for advice on composing an appropriate message to read for the mission's telecast. Not only would it be the first ever from the moon, but it also fell on Christmas Eve. After discussing it with friends, Bourgin came back to Borman with an answer: a reading from Genesis.

This, Bourgin explained, "would sound the universal appeal and sense of reverence that is called for." He continued, "these simple words from the Bible spoken feelingly and simply by you could only be accepted as a sincere expression of one human being to his fellows, and truly reflect the humility that the occasion must register." Borman took Bourgin's advice.

At the end of one of the most tumultuous years in history, with the assassinations of Martin Luther King, Jr., and Robert F. Kennedy, war in Vietnam, and protests around the nation, the Apollo 8 crew took turns reading the first 10 verses of Genesis. Borman ended the telecast with the now famous line Bourgin suggested: "Good night, good luck, a Merry Christmas, and God bless you all—all of you on the good Earth."

49 Australian Television Network Boomerang

Date: ca 1969
Manufacturer: Unknown
Origin: Australia
Materials: Wood, with metal citation plate
Dimensions: 30 by 3 inches

As the Apollo 11 motorcade made its way through the streets of Perth on October 31, 1969, the song "Happy Birthday" rang out for astronaut Michael Collins, who was celebrating his 39th birthday on this leg of the crew's worldwide postflight goodwill tour. Among the many commemorative gifts the crew received, an iconic one from the Australian Television Network stood out: the "first aerodynamic shape conceived by man," also known as a boomerang (opposite).

The tour followed a grueling schedule. After the astronauts arrived in a country, they attended event after event with very few pauses before leaving for the next nation. In Australia, the astronauts visited two cities, an extra stop that reflected that country's essential role in the first lunar landing: enabling the entire world to watch the flight live on television.

In the late 1950s, NASA started building up a worldwide network of tracking stations for communications with orbiting spacecraft. Because Australia is roughly 180° longitude from Cape Canaveral, Florida, it became a geographically strategic location for supporting the U.S. space program. As spacecraft passed over Australia, with the aid of the tracking stations, NASA could confirm the entry into orbit as well as send instructions to the capsule.

To receive TV transmissions during Project Apollo, NASA arranged a system of three stations around the world distanced approximately 120 degrees

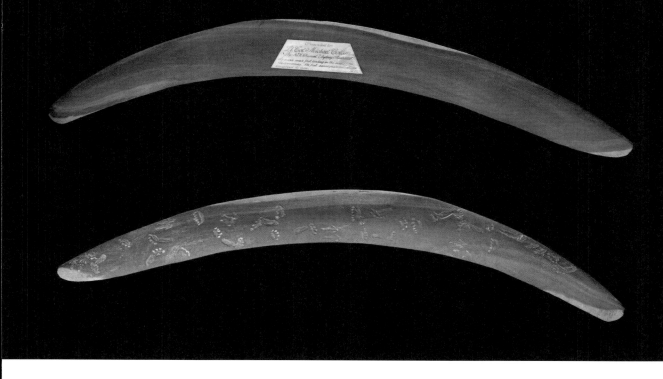

from each other, to ensure a station was always facing the moon. These three stations—Goldstone, California, United States; Madrid, Spain; and Honeysuckle Creek, Australia—served as relay points between the Apollo crews and Mission Control in Houston, Texas. Unlike earlier tracking stations, they were equipped with the new Unified S-band communication system, able to send and receive data through one 26-meter antenna rather than multiple separate radio links. NASA would select the best quality image feed to be broadcast to television sets around the world.

The Honeysuckle Creek Tracking Station, located outside Canberra in a mountainous region of southeastern Australia, opened in March 1967. In New South Wales, the preexisting Parkes Radio Telescope, with a 64-meter antenna, served as a backup. NASA designed the system so that the signal from the moon would be routed through Honeysuckle Creek and Parkes to Sydney via microwave link. From Sydney, the signal traveled to Mission Control in Houston via the INTEL-SAT geostationary communications satellite over the Pacific Ocean, and directly to the Australian Broadcasting Commission studios for distribution to Australian television networks.

When the LM *Eagle* landed on the lunar surface on July 20, 1969, the

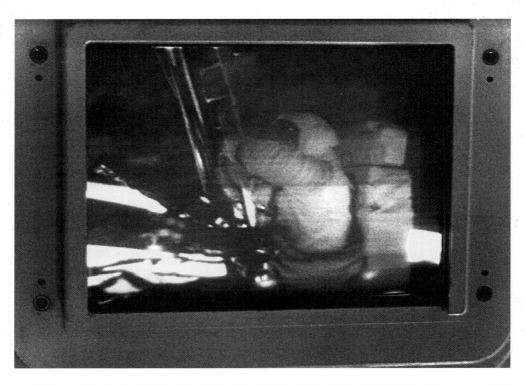

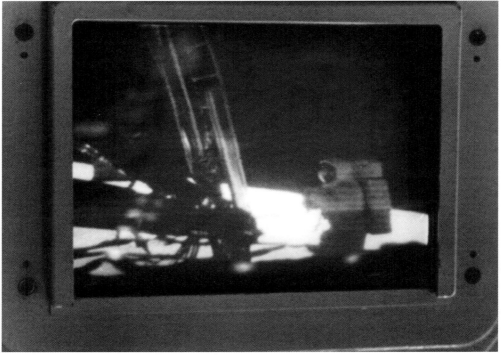

PAGE 285: Michael Collins received this gift from the Australian Television Network Channel 7 with the inscription "To mark man's first landing on the moon—this boomerang, the first aerodynamic shape conceived by man."

OPPOSITE: Unconverted slow-scan TV images of Neil Armstrong attaching his camera to its suit mount (top) and guiding Buzz Aldrin down the ladder (bottom).

Goldstone Tracking Station in California beamed its TV signal to a worldwide audience. As the astronauts suited up for their extravehicular activity (EVA), deciding to forgo their scheduled rest period, Earth rotated, and Australia began to face the moon. Armstrong deployed the television camera that would record the first steps on the lunar surface, which sent a signal to Earth. Madrid was well out of range, Parkes just slightly, and the Goldstone feed was heavily distorted. So NASA selected the Honeysuckle Creek transmission for the beginning of the television broadcast.

Ed von Renouard, a technician there, recalled: "When the image first appeared in front of me it was an indecipherable puzzle of stark blocks of black at the bottom and gray at the top, bisected by a bright diagonal streak. I realized that the sky should be at the top, and on the moon, the sky is black, so I reached out and flicked the switch and all of a sudden it all made sense, and presently Armstrong's leg came down." When Parkes started receiving a signal from *Eagle* that was much clearer, NASA switched to the Parkes TV transmission for the remainder of the broadcast. As a result, when a fifth of the world's population—over half a billion people—watched Armstrong and Aldrin on the moon, they were watching a feed routed through Australian observatories. And Australian audiences had the distinct privilege of witnessing the first steps on the moon 0.3 seconds ahead of the rest of the world because their television feed did not have to travel up to INTELSAT and then to Houston before lighting up their television sets.

Collins, who became director of the Smithsonian National Air and Space Museum in 1971, later donated this boomerang, as well as other personal artifacts, to the national collection. It memorializes the close relationship between the United States and Australia in the history of spaceflight. •

50 Apollo 11 F-1 Engine Parts

Date: 1968
Manufacturer: Rocketdyne,
Division, North American Rockwell
Origin: Los Angeles, California
Materials: CRES steel, copper,
aluminum, Teflon, Inconel X
Original dimensions: 18 feet $4^{15}/_{16}$
inches long; 12 feet $^5/_{16}$ inch
diameter

The components of the F-1 engines that propelled Neil Armstrong, Buzz Aldrin, and Mike Collins to the moon in 1969 now bear evidence of a fierce impact with the surface of the Atlantic Ocean and about 40 years spent on the ocean floor. Together, five F-1s sat at the base of the first stage of the Saturn V rocket, the 138-foot-tall S-IC. When the S-IC stage was exhausted, it fell away and landed in the Atlantic Ocean at a speed of roughly 200 miles an hour. The stage, along with the F-1 engines, sank 14,000 feet to the ocean floor, where they would remain until 2013.

With 1.5 million pounds of thrust, the F-1 engine was the most powerful single-nozzle, liquid-fueled rocket engine in history. Engineers at Rocketdyne first conceived of the engine in 1955, two years before any human-made object orbited in space. After NASA's creation in 1958, the agency revived the F-1 engine concept, and Rocketdyne tested the first full-size prototype in 1961. The design of the F-1 was a scaled-up version of the company's other engines, but fabrication of the massive engine required new manufacturing and testing techniques. Each engine consumed 6,000 pounds of RP-1, a form of kerosene, and liquid oxygen every second. Five F-1 engines clustered together launched the massive Saturn V into space with 7.5 million pounds of thrust at liftoff. Launch after launch, F-1s propelled all the lunar missions without failure.

More than 40 years after the first lunar landing, Jeff Bezos, founder of Amazon and the aerospace company Blue Origin, wondered if "with the right team of undersea pros, could we find and potentially recover the F-1 engines that started mankind's mission to the moon?" In 2011 he created Bezos Expeditions to seek out and recover the F-1 components from the ocean floor. The team searched an area of one nautical mile along the Apollo 11 flight path using deep-sea sonar. For nearly three weeks, they retrieved thrust chambers, gas generators, injectors, heat exchangers, turbopumps, fuel manifolds, and other hardware, all deformed, but recognizable as parts from the Apollo moon missions.

Bezos Expeditions sent the recovered components to the Kansas Cosmosphere and Space Center (KCSC) for conservation. Instead of restoring the pieces to their original launch condition, conservators stabilized the artifacts and removed corrosion. As Jim Remar, president and chief executive officer of the KCSC, explained, "The artifacts have a story and life. We didn't want to do anything that changed their look or appearance because we felt that would take away some of the story." During the stabilization process, the conservators found markings proving that some of these components were part of Apollo 11.

These artifacts return us to the central focus of this book: how artifacts have been, and continue to be, essential connections to the past.

When asked why he recovered the F-1 engine parts, Jeff Bezos offered an explanation. "Millions of people were inspired by the Apollo Program. I was five years old when I watched Apollo 11 unfold on television, and without any doubt, it was a big contributor to my passions for science, engineering, and exploration." Bezos worked with NASA to make the Apollo 11 F-1 engine components available to the Smithsonian National Air and Space Museum, in the hope that they could once again inspire future generations.

Why preserve the artifacts of spaceflight? Why do physical remnants of history matter to us? Why did Neil Armstrong bring pieces of the Wright Flyer to the moon?

Now that the Apollo 11 F-1 engine parts are on dry land, they can once again be part of our lives. They have the power to create new experiences and inspire new generations. Like other

OPPOSITE, TOP: Remotely operated underwater vehicles filmed the thrust chamber and fuel manifold of an F-1 engine on the ocean floor.

OPPOSITE, BOTTOM: Crew of the Norwegian salvage vessel *Seabed Worker* raise and secure the F-1 thrust chamber on deck.

"I was five years old when I watched Apollo 11 unfold on television, and without any doubt, it was a big contributor to my passions for science, engineering, and exploration."

—Jeff Bezos, founder of Amazon and the aerospace company Blue Origins

artifacts, the F-1 engine components carry marks of their history. Before they were launched, the F-1 engines impressed with their scale and intricate design, but the flown engine parts communicate something different. These battered fragments bear witness to the repercussions of a journey to the moon. You can experience the immense size, the tremendous forces they were subjected to, and the significant risks inherent in launching—and riding—a spacecraft to the moon. You can see the damage from their ocean impact and the corrosion from years underwater. They connect us to Project Apollo; to the engineers who designed, tested, and built them; to the astronauts who flew to the moon; to the crew who recovered them; and to the conservators who stabilized them for years to come.

Just as Armstrong connected his experience to the Wright brothers' flight with the shard of wood and piece of fabric, Apollo artifacts can connect us to the first moon missions. The F-1 engine parts, like the Wright Flyer pieces and the other artifacts in this book, or the thousands more at the Smithsonian Institution, have the power to render lunar exploration tangible instead of abstract. Artifacts make Project Apollo more than memory alone; they make it a palpable, and visitable, part of our present. •

To the Moon

APOLLO TIME LINE

AS-201

Launch Date: 2/26/1966
Splashdown Date: 2/26/1966
Mission Duration: 0:37:19
Launch Vehicle: SA-201
Command Module No.: 9
Mission Summary: The first launch of the Block I Apollo CSM

AS-203

Launch Date: 7/5/1966
Launch Vehicle: SA-203
Mission Summary: A test of the S-IVB rocket, with no spacecraft

AS-202

Launch Date: 8/25/1966
Splashdown Date: 8/25/1966
Mission Duration: 1:32:02
Launch Vehicle: SA-202
Command Module No.: 11
Mission Summary: Another test of the Block I CSM, and the first flight to include the Apollo Primary Guidance, Navigation and Control System

"Apollo 1"

Launch Date: N/A
Splashdown Date: N/A
Launch Vehicle: AS-204
Command Module No.: 12
Crew: Virgil "Gus" Grissom; Edward H. White II; Roger B. Chaffee
Mission Summary: First crewed test of Block I Apollo hardware. Crew perished on January 27, 1967, during a preflight test, prompting a redesign of the Apollo spacecraft. The spacecraft was retroactively designated "Apollo 1" later that year.

Apollo 4

Launch Date: 11/9/1967
Splashdown Date: 11/9/1967
Mission Duration: 08:36:59
Launch Vehicle: AS-501
Command Module No.: 17

Lunar Module No.: Lunar Module Test Article 10R
Mission Summary: First Saturn V launch, and at the time the largest thing to have ever flown

Apollo 5

Launch Date: 1/22/1968
Splashdown Date: N/A
Mission Duration: 11:10:00
Launch Vehicle: SA-204
Lunar Module No.: 1
Mission Summary: The first test of the lunar module in Earth orbit

Apollo 6

Launch Date: 4/4/1968
Splashdown Date: 4/4/1968
Mission Duration: 9:50:00
Launch Vehicle: AS-502
Command Module No.: 20
Lunar Module No.: Lunar Module Test Article 2R
Mission Summary: Final uncrewed test with all spacecraft components except for a working LM

Apollo 7

Launch Date: 10/11/1968
Splashdown Date: 10/22/1968
Mission Duration: 260:09:03
Launch Vehicle: SA-205
Command Module No., Call Sign: 101, "Apollo 7"
Crew: Walter "Wally" M. Schirra, commander; Donn F. Eisele, command module pilot; Ronnie "Ron" Walter Cunningham, lunar module pilot
Mission Summary: First crewed engineering test flight of Block II Apollo craft. Demonstrated craft, crew, and mission capabilities during an Earth orbital flight. Though it never left Earth orbit, it traveled a greater distance than any other command module.

Apollo 8

Launch Date: 12/21/1968
Splashdown Date: 12/27/1968
Mission Duration: 147:00:42

Launch Vehicle: AS-503
Command Module No., Call Sign: 103, "Apollo 8"
Crew: Frank Borman, commander; James A. Lovell, Jr., command module pilot; William A. Anders, lunar module pilot
Mission Summary: The first crewed mission to orbit the moon, and return to Earth

Apollo 9

Launch Date: 3/3/1969
Splashdown Date: 3/13/1969
Mission Duration: 241:00:54
Launch Vehicle: AS-504
Command Module No., Call Sign: 104, *Gumdrop*
Lunar Module No., Call Sign: 3, *Spider*
Crew: James A. McDivitt, commander; David R. Scott, command module pilot; Russell L. Schweickart, lunar module pilot
Mission Summary: The first crewed test of the lunar module in Earth orbit, proving the lunar orbital rendezvous plan

Apollo 10

Launch Date: 5/18/1969
Splashdown Date: 5/26/1969
Mission Duration: 192:03:23
Launch Vehicle: AS-505
Command Module No., Call Sign: 106, *Charlie Brown*
Lunar Module No., Call Sign: 4, *Snoopy*
Crew: Thomas P. Stafford, commander; John W. Young, command module pilot; Eugene A. Cernan, lunar module pilot
Mission Summary: First test of the lunar module in lunar orbit, including a test of the entire mission plan short of actual lunar landing. During the return to Earth, it achieved the fastest speed humans have ever traveled.

Apollo 11

Launch Date: 7/16/1969
Splashdown Date: 7/24/1969
Mission Duration: 195:18:35

Launch Vehicle: AS-506
Command Module No., Call Sign: 107, *Columbia*
Lunar Module No., Call Sign: 5, *Eagle*
Lunar Surface Dates: 7/20–7/21
Landing Site: Sea of Tranquility
Total Lunar Surface Time: 21:36:21
Total Lunar EVA Time: 1 EVA: 2:31:40
Crew: Neil A. Armstrong, commander; Michael Collins, command module pilot; Edwin E. "Buzz" Aldrin, Jr., lunar module pilot
Mission Summary: First lunar landing and moonwalk

Apollo 12

Launch Date: 11/14/1969
Splashdown Date: 11/24/1969
Mission Duration: 244:36:25
Launch Vehicle: AS-507
Command Module No., Call Sign: 108, *Yankee Clipper*
Lunar Module No., Call Sign: 6, *Intrepid*
Lunar Surface Dates: 11/19–11/20
Landing Site: Ocean of Storms
Total Lunar Surface Time: 31:31:12
Total Lunar EVA Time: 2 EVAs: 7:45:18
Crew: Charles "Pete" Conrad, Jr., commander; Richard F. Gordon, Jr., command module pilot; Alan L. Bean, lunar module pilot
Mission Summary: Lunar landing, deployment of lunar experiments, and the first human visit to a space probe, Surveyor 3

Apollo 13

Launch Date: 4/11/1970
Splashdown Date: 4/17/1970
Mission Duration: 142:54:41
Launch Vehicle: AS-508
Command Module No., Call Sign: 109, *Odyssey*
Lunar Module No., Call Sign: 7, *Aquarius*
Crew: James A. Lovell, commander; John L. Swigert, Jr., command module pilot; Fred W. Haise, lunar module pilot
Mission Summary: An explosion in flight resulted in the crew using the lunar module as a lifeboat, while returning to Earth after a lunar slingshot maneuver.

Apollo 14

Launch Date: 1/31/1971
Splashdown Date: 2/9/1971
Mission Duration: 216:01:58
Launch Vehicle: AS-509
Command Module No., Call Sign: 110, *Kitty Hawk*
Lunar Module No., Call Sign: 8, *Antares*
Lunar Surface Dates: 2/5–2/6
Landing Site: Fra Mauro
Total Lunar Surface Time: 33:30:31
Total Lunar EVA Time: 2 EVAs: 9:22:31
Crew: Alan B. Shepard, Jr., commander; Stuart A. Roosa, command module pilot; Edgar D. Mitchell, lunar module pilot
Mission Summary: Repeated the mission plan for Apollo 13: deployed experiments and took photographs of future landing sites

Apollo 15

Launch Date: 7/26/1971
Splashdown Date: 8/7/1971
Mission Duration: 295:11:53
Launch Vehicle: AS-510
Command Module No., Call Sign: 112, *Endeavour*
Lunar Module No., Call Sign: 10, *Falcon*
Lunar Surface Dates: 7/30–8/2
Landing Site: Hadley-Apennine
Total Lunar Surface Time: 66:54:53
Total Lunar EVA Time: 3 EVAs: 18:34:46
Crew: David R. Scott, commander; Alfred M. Worden, command module pilot; James B. Irwin, lunar module pilot
Mission Summary: First usage of the lunar roving vehicle to extend range of sample collection; also included first use of the service module science bay, the first deployment of a satellite into lunar orbit from a spacecraft, and first deep-space EVA

Apollo 16

Launch Date: 4/16/1972
Splashdown Date: 4/27/1972
Mission Duration: 265:51:05
Launch Vehicle: AS-511
Command Module No., Call Sign: 113, *Casper*
Lunar Module No., Call Sign: 11, *Orion*
Lunar Surface Dates: 4/21–4/23
Landing Site: Descartes Highlands
Total Lunar Surface Time: 71:02:13
Total Lunar EVA Time: 3 EVAs: 20:14:14
Crew: John W. Young, commander; Thomas K. Mattingly II, command module pilot; Charles M. Duke, Jr., lunar module pilot
Mission Summary: The first mission to explore the hilly, rough lunar highlands, thought to be more characteristic of the majority of the moon's surface than other landing sites; also the first and only mission to conduct ultraviolet photographic astronomy on the moon's surface

Apollo 17

Launch Date: 12/7/1972
Splashdown Date: 12/19/1972
Mission Duration: 301:51:59
Launch Vehicle: AS-512
Command Module No., Call Sign: 114, *America*
Lunar Module No., Call Sign: 12, *Challenger*
Lunar Surface Dates: 12/11–12/14
Landing Site: Taurus-Littrow
Total Lunar Surface Time: 74:59:40
Total Lunar EVA Time: 3 EVAs: 22:03:57
Crew: Eugene A. Cernan, commander; Ronald E. Evans, command module pilot; Harrison H. "Jack" Schmitt, lunar module pilot
Mission Summary: The last Apollo mission and last moonwalk to date; included the first scientist on the moon

Further Reading

Aldrin, Buzz, and Ken Abraham, *Magnificent Desolation: The Long Journey Home From the Moon* (New York: Three Rivers Press, 2010).

Beattie, Donald, *Taking Science to the Moon: Lunar Experiments and the Apollo Program* (Baltimore: Johns Hopkins University Press, 2001).

Bilstein, Roger, *Stages to Saturn: A Technological History of the Apollo/Saturn Launch Vehicles* (Gainesville: University Press of Florida, 2003).

Borman, Frank, and Robert J. Serling, *Countdown: An Autobiography* (New York: William Morrow, 1988).

Chaikin, Andrew, *A Man on the Moon: The Voyages of the Apollo Astronauts* (New York: Viking, 1994).

Collins, Martin, and Sylvia Fries, eds., *A Spacefaring Nation: Perspectives on American Space History and Policy* (Washington, D.C.: Smithsonian Institution Press, 1991).

Collins, Martin, and Douglas Millard, eds., *Showcasing Space* (East Lansing: Michigan State University Press, 2005).

Collins, Michael, *Carrying the Fire: An Astronaut's Journeys* (New York: Farrar, Straus, and Giroux, 1974).

Columbia Broadcasting System, *10:56:20 PM EDT, 7/20/69: The Historic Conquest of the Moon as Reported to the American People* (New York: Columbia Broadcasting System, 1970).

Cosgrove, Denis. *Apollo's Eye: A Cartographic Genealogy of the Earth in the Western Imagination* (Baltimore: Johns Hopkins University Press, 2003).

Dean, James, and Bertram Ulrich, *NASA/ART: 50 Years of Exploration* (New York: Abrams, 2008).

Dick, Steven J., ed., *Remembering the Space Age* (Washington, D.C.: NASA History Division, 2008).

Dick, Steven J., and Roger D. Launius, eds., *Critical Issues in the History of Spaceflight* (Washington, D.C.: NASA History Division, 2006).

———, *Societal Impact of Spaceflight* (Washington, D.C.: NASA History Division, 2007).

Hacker, Barton, and James Grimwood, *On the Shoulders of Titans: A History of Project Gemini* (Washington, D.C.: NASA, 1977).

Hansen, James, *First Man: The Life of Neil A. Armstrong* (New York: Simon and Schuster, 2005).

Harland, David, *Exploring the Moon: The Apollo Expeditions* (New York: Springer, 1999).

Hersch, Matthew H., *Inventing the American Astronaut* (New York: Palgrave Macmillan, 2012).

Johnson, Stephen B., *The Secret of Apollo: Systems Management in American and European Space Programs* (Baltimore: Johns Hopkins University Press, 2002).

Kelly, Thomas, *Moon Lander: How We Developed the Apollo Lunar Module* (Washington, D.C.: Smithsonian Institution Press, 2001).

Kraft, Christopher, *Flight: My Life in Mission Control* (New York: Dutton, 2001).

Kranz, Gene, *Failure Is Not an Option: Mission Control From Mercury to Apollo 13 and Beyond* (New York: Simon and Schuster, 2000).

Krige, John, Angelina Long Callahan, and Ashok Maharaj, *NASA in the World: Fifty Years of International Collaboration in Space* (New York: Palgrave Macmillan, 2013).

Lambright, W. Henry, *Powering Apollo: James E. Webb of NASA* (Baltimore: Johns Hopkins University Press, 1998).

Launius, Roger D., and Dennis Jenkins, *Coming Home: Reentry and Recovery From Space* (Washington, D.C.: NASA Aeronautics Book Series, 2012).

Launius, Roger D., and Howard E. McCurdy, eds., *Spaceflight and the Myth of Presidential Leadership* (Urbana: University of Illinois Press, 1997).

Launius, Roger D., John Logsdon, and Robert W. Smith, eds., *Reconsidering Sputnik: Forty Years Since the Soviet Satellite* (Australia: Harwood Academic, 2000).

Levasseur, Jennifer, *Pictures by Proxy: Images of Exploration and the First Decade of Astronaut Photography at NASA* (Ph.D. diss., History, George Mason University, 2014).

Lewis, Cathleen, *The Red Stuff: A History of the Public and Material Culture of Early Human Spaceflight in the U.S.S.R.* (Ph.D. diss., History, George Washington University, 2008).

Logsdon, John, *The Decision to Go to the Moon: Project Apollo and the National Interest* (Cambridge, MA: MIT Press, 1970).

———, *John F. Kennedy and the Race to the Moon* (New York: Palgrave Macmillan, 2011).

Logsdon, John, and Roger D. Launius, eds., *Exploring the Unknown: Selected Documents in the History of the U.S. Civil Space Program, Volume VII: Human Spaceflight: Projects Mercury, Gemini, and Apollo* (Washington, D.C.: NASA History Division, 2008).

Lovell, James, and Jeffrey Kluger, *Lost Moon: The Perilous Voyage of Apollo 13* (New York: Houghton Mifflin, 1994).

Maher, Neil, *Apollo in the Age of Aquarius* (Cambridge, MA: Harvard University Press, 2017).

McCray, W. Patrick, *Keep Watching the Skies!: The Story of Operation Moonwatch and the Dawn of the Space Age* (Princeton, NJ: Princeton University Press, 2008).

McCurdy, Howard, *Space and the American Imagination* (Washington, D.C.: Smithsonian Institution Press, 1999).

McDougall, Walter A., *. . . The Heavens and the Earth: A Political History of the Space Age* (New York: Basic Books, 1985).

Mindell, David, *Digital Apollo: Human and Machine in Spaceflight* (Cambridge, MA: MIT Press, 2008).

Monchaux, Nicholas de, *Spacesuit: Fashioning Apollo* (Cambridge, MA: MIT Press, 2011).

Murray, Charles A., and Catherine Bly Cox, *Apollo: The Race to the Moon* (New York: Simon and Schuster, 1989).

Neufeld, Michael, *Von Braun: Dreamer of Space, Engineer of War* (New York: Knopf, 2007).

Paul, Richard, and Steven Moss, *We Could Not Fail: The First African Americans in the Space Program* (Austin: University of Texas Press, 2015).

Poole, Robert, *Earthrise: How Man First Saw the Earth* (New Haven, CT: Yale University Press, 2008).

Schwoch, James, *Global TV: New Media and the Cold War, 1946–69* (Champaign: University of Illinois Press, 2008).

Scott, David Meerman, and Richard Jurek, *Marketing the Moon: The Selling of the Apollo Lunar Program* (Cambridge, MA: MIT Press, 2014).

Siddiqi, Asif, *Challenge to Apollo: The Soviet Union and the Space Race, 1945–1974* (Washington, D.C.: NASA History Division, 2000).

———, *The Red Rockets' Glare: Spaceflight and the Soviet Imagination, 1857–1957* (New York: Cambridge University Press, 2010).

Swenson, Loyd, James Grimwood, and Charles Alexander, *This New Ocean: A History of Project Mercury* (Washington, D.C.: NASA, 1998).

Tribbe, Matthew D., *No Requiem for the Space Age: The Apollo Moon Landings and American Culture* (New York: Oxford University Press, 2014).

Weitekamp, Margaret A., *Right Stuff, Wrong Sex: America's First Women in Space Program* (Baltimore: Johns Hopkins University Press, 2004).

Online Resources

Apollo Flight Journal *(https://history.nasa.gov/afj)*

Apollo Lunar Surface Journal *(www.hq.nasa.gov/alsj)*

Johnson Space Center Oral History Project *(www.jsc.nasa.gov/history/oral_histories/oral_histories.htm)*

About the Authors

Teasel Muir-Harmony, curator at the Smithsonian National Air and Space Museum, is a distinguished scholar of space history. She earned a Ph.D. from Massachusetts Institute of Technology, writing a dissertation on the political implications of the Apollo program. She has published more than a dozen articles and book reviews and has presented internationally on various topics in the cultural history of 20th-century space science.

Michael Collins was a NASA astronaut from 1963 to 1970. He flew into space twice, first as a pilot for Gemini 10 in 1966 and second as the command module pilot for Apollo 11. Collins served as the director of the Smithsonian National Air and Space Museum from 1971 to 1978.

Guest Contributors

David DeVorkin, senior curator, Smithsonian National Air and Space Museum
    #34: Carruthers's Far Ultraviolet Camera/ Spectrograph
    George R. Carruthers, Aerospace Engineer

Meghann Girard, Engen Preprogram Conservation Fellow, Smithsonian National Air and Space Museum
    #39: Command Module Medical Kit, Apollo 11

Jennifer Levasseur, museum curator, Smithsonian National Air and Space Museum
    #25: Hasselblad Camera, Apollo 17

Allan Needell, museum curator, Smithsonian National Air and Space Museum
    #38: Block I Inner Hatch, Apollo 4
    #47: The Armstrong Purse, Apollo 11

Michael Neufeld, senior curator, Smithsonian National Air and Space Museum
    Wernher von Braun and the Development of Rocketry

Matthew Sanders, museum researcher, Smithsonian National Air and Space Museum
    #3: Project Moonwatch Telescope
    Margaret Hamilton, Lead Apollo Flight Software Designer
    #13: Saturn V Instrument Unit
    #19: Crawler-Transporter Tread
    And substantial contributions to additional essays

Matthew Shindell, museum curator, Smithsonian National Air and Space Museum
    #32: Camera, Surveyor 3 Spacecraft

Priscilla Strain, program manager, Smithsonian National Air and Space Museum
    Farouk El-Baz, Lunar Geologist

John Tylko, Aurora Flight Sciences and Massachusetts Institute of Technology
    #9: Apollo Guidance Computer
    #10: Apollo Mission Simulators

Acknowledgments

This book owes much to my fellow curators in the Space History Department, who reviewed every essay in this volume, offering invaluable edits, insights, and collegiality; to Nick Partridge, who guided the project from proposal to completion; to Kate Bulson, who is responsible for the eye-catching images throughout these pages; and to the unstinting support and skill of the National Geographic team: Susan Hitchcock, Michelle Cassidy, Katie Olsen, and Melissa Farris.

I am also indebted to many colleagues and friends who were remarkably generous with their time and expertise: the Piqua Public Library Archives and Special Collections; Jennifer Ross-Nazzal at NASA's Johnson Space Center Archives; Jim Remar and Shannon Whetzel of the Cosmosphere; Elizabeth Suckow and Colin Fries from the NASA Headquarters History Division; Paul Dauber and Jeremy Litek, for supplying Bezos Expeditions images; Sarah Foster-Chang; Claire Jerry; Melissa Keiser, Kate Igoe, and Allan Janus of the NASM Archives, for finding and scanning all manner of images and documents; Eric Long and Patrick Leonini, for finding and taking photos; Carolyn Russo and Tom Crouch, for assistance with NASA Art; Toby Ellman; Kunie Fujiki DeVorkin, for translation help; Rebecca Dobrow; Claire Scoville; Lilia Teal; and the Apollo Lunar Surface Journal and Apollo Flight Journal for invaluable resources.

I am deeply grateful to Mike Collins for writing the foreword, as well as for his immense contribution to Project Apollo and the preservation of the program's artifacts. I could not have completed this book without Matt Sanders's dogged research, enviable sleuthing skills, and good cheer. A better research assistant is impossible to find. Finally, thanks are always due to my loved ones, the marvelous Michael, Rebecca, Ayr, Brooke, Clementine, Blue, Violet, Asa, Amos, Arla, Ace, and Zeke. *Apollo to the Moon* is dedicated to my brother-in-law Alex, an endless source of good ideas—like the idea for this book.

 # Illustrations Credits

All photographs in this book come from the collection of Smithsonian National Air and Space Museum. Additional credits below.

Cover, NASA; 2-3, Apollo 17 Crew, NASA; Panorama Assembly: Mike Constantine; 4, NASA; 9, NASA; 10 (UP), AP Photo; 10 (LO), AP/Shutterstock; 18-19, NASA; 23, NASA; 28, U.S. Navy photo courtesy NASA; 35 (LO), Smithsonian National Postal Museum; 36, Fine Art Images/Heritage Images/Getty Images; 39, AP Photo; 40-43, Smithsonian National Museum of American History; 44, NASA; 48, NASA; 55 (BOTH), NASA; 59, John F. Kennedy Presidential Library and Museum; 62, Smithsonian National Postal Museum; 63, NASA; 67, NASA; 68, Courtesy MIT Museum; 71, NASA; 76-7, NASA; 85, NASA; 86, NASA; 90, NASA/MSFC; 92, NASA; 101, NASA; 102, NASA; 103 (LO), NASA; 107, NASA; 110, Walter A. Weber/National Geographic Creative; 113 (ALL), NASA; 123, Thomas Usciak; 126, NASA; 131, Bettmann/Getty Images; 135, NASA; 140, NASA; 142, NASA photo courtesy The Piqua Public Library Archives and Special Collections; 147, NASA; 154-5 (ALL), www.exergenie.com *EXER-GENIE*® is a Registered Trademark of Team America Health & Fitness, Inc. All Rights Reserved 1962–2018; 158, NASA; 163, NG Maps; 167, CBS Photo Archive/Getty Images; 170 (ALL), NASA; 175, Sovfoto/UIG via Getty Images; 178-9, NASA; 183, NASA; 184 (ALL), NASA; 188, NASA; 193, NASA; 197, NASA; 200-201, NASA; 202, NASA; 206, NASA; 208, NASA; 212, NASA; 215 (UP RT), NASA; 215 (CTR RT), NASA; 215 (LO RT), NASA; 216 (BOTH), NASA; 218, NASA; 222, NASA; 235, Courtesy Meghann Kozak; 239 (BOTH), NASA; 243, NASA/Science Source/Getty Images; 247, NASA; 250-51, NASA; 252, NASA; 254-5, NASA; 255 (BOTH), Richard Nixon Presidential Library and Museum; 259, NASA; 263, NASA; 264-5, NASA; 267, NASA; 272, NASA; 275, Copyright, all rights reserved. Courtesy of the Smithsonian's National Air and Space Museum; 277, NASA; 281, AP Photo; 282, Courtesy Cecilia Rolando; 286 (BOTH), Courtesy honeysucklecreek.net; 289, NASA; 290, NASA; 293 (BOTH), © 2013 Bezos Expeditions | www.bezosexpeditions.com/engine-recovery.html

Index

Boldface indicates illustrations.

Since 1888, the National Geographic Society has funded more than 13,000 research, exploration, and preservation projects around the world. National Geographic Partners distributes a portion of the funds it receives from your purchase to National Geographic Society to support programs including the conservation of animals and their habitats.

National Geographic Partners
1145 17th Street NW
Washington, DC 20036-4688 USA

Get closer to National Geographic explorers and photographers, and connect with our global community. Join us today at nationalgeographic.com/join

For information about special discounts for bulk purchases, please contact National Geographic Books Special Sales: specialsales@natgeo.com

For rights or permissions inquiries, please contact National Geographic Books Subsidiary Rights: bookrights@natgeo.com

ISBN: 978-1-4262-1993-1
ISBN: 978-1-4262-2025-8 (special edition)

Printed in China

18/RRDS/1

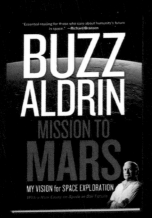

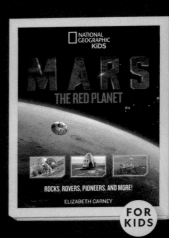
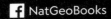 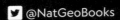